Planning
for the Early Years
Foundation Stage

Planning for the Early Years Foundation Stage complements the six learning area books in this series by explaining the basis of clear planning and how it links to careful observation and assessment. Useful examples are provided throughout. Planning across the Early Years Foundation Stage will raise awareness of what is needed within early years' settings, explain the who, when and why of observation, assessment and planning, and make useful links to each of the other books in the series.

Sandra Smidt is a writer and consultant in Early Years education.

Practical Guidance in the EYFS
Series Editor: Sandy Green

The *Practical Guidance in the EYFS* series will assist practitioners in the smooth and successful implementation of the Early Years Foundation Stage.

Each book gives clear and detailed explanations of each aspect of learning and development and encourages readers to consider each area within its broadest context to expand and develop their own knowledge and good practice.

Practical ideas and activities for all age groups are offered along with a wealth of expertise of how elements from the practice guidance can be implemented within all early years' settings. The books include suggestions for the innovative use of everyday resources, popular books and stories.

Titles in this series include:

Planning
for the Early Years
Foundation Stage

Sandra Smidt

Routledge
Taylor & Francis Group

LONDON AND NEW YORK

First published 2009
by Routledge
2 Park Square, Milton Park, Abingdon, Oxon OX14 4RN

Simultaneously published in the USA and Canada
by Routledge
270 Madison Avenue, New York, NY 10016

Reprinted 2009 (twice), 2010 (twice)

Routledge is an imprint of the Taylor & Francis Group, an informa business

Typeset in Optima by
Taylor & Francis Books
Printed and bound in Great Britain by
TJ International Ltd, Padstow, Cornwall

British Library Cataloguing in Publication Data
A catalogue record for this book is available from the British Library

Library of Congress Cataloging in Publication Data
Smidt, Sandra, 1943–
    Planning for the early years foundation stage / Sandra Smidt.
        p. cm. – (Practical guidance in the EYFS)
    Includes bibliographical references and index.
    1. Early childhood education. 2. Early childhood education–Curricula.
    3. Child development. 4. Education, Preschool. I. Title.
    LB1139.23.S65 2009
372.21–dc22   2008043737

ISBN 978-0-415-47839-7 (hbk)
ISBN 978-0-415-47729-1 (pbk)

The photographs in this book are of my grandchildren when they were much younger than they are now: Hannah, Ben, Chloe, Jacob and Zac.

Contents

Acronyms

Titles in the *Practical Guidance in the EYFS* series:

PSED   *Personal, Social and Emotional Development*

CLL   *Communication, Language and Literacy*

KUW   *Knowledge and Understanding of the World*

CD   *Creative Development*

PSRN   *Problem Solving, Reasoning and Numeracy*

PD   *Physical Development*

Introduction

This book is the last in a series of books looking at the implications of the new Early Years Foundation Stage which became mandatory from September 2008 for all those in schools and other early years OFSTED-registered settings attended by children from birth to the end of the academic year in which they turn five. The first six books look at how to offer learning opportunities across the age ranges involved (namely from birth–20 months, 16–36 months and 30–60+ months) and each book addresses this in one of the six specified learning areas. Each book looks at storybooks, activities or learning stories as a starting point and each is rich in details of possible activities, suggestions of what to look out for, how to plan and resource, how to ensure your practice is effective and how to take account of making links with homes and cultures. This book takes a broader view and looks at planning in a more general and sometimes theoretical sense, and in doing this includes some reference to the work of each of the six other authors in the series. Look out for the symbols alerting you to the other titles: *Personal, Social and Emotional Development* (PSED) by Sue Sheppy; *Communication, Language and Literacy* (CLL) by Helen Bradford: *Knowledge and Understanding of the World* (KUW) by Stella Louis; *Creative Development* (CD) by Pamela May; *Problem Solving, Reasoning and Numeracy* (PSRN) by Anita M. Hughes; and *Physical Development* (PD) by Angela D. Nurse.

    In this book the convention of using 'she' rather than 'he' when talking about individuals has been adopted. This overcomes the more clumsy conventions of using 'he/she' or 'his/hers' or the alternative of alternating 'he' and 'she' in each paragraph.

    At the end of each chapter you will find a glossary of terms which may be unfamiliar or unclear to you. To help you some of the terms which will be included in the glossary are in **bold** the first time they appear in the text. The glossary takes the form of the glossary term in bold followed by an explanation of that term for those involved in early education and care.

I am grateful for the opportunity offered by Birgit Voss to visit the Andover Early Years Centre in Islington, London, where I was able to see the effects of careful, sensitive and child-focused planning in action and where the Profile books I was shown gave me a real picture of individual children's day by day progress over time, charting sometimes tiny and sometimes startling leaps in learning and development. What I found reassuring in these books were the 'voices' of the staff, of the children themselves and of their parents, which were to be found on the pages of the books through the comments made, the examples of what children had done and the photographs of the children sharing these books with parents, key workers and peers.

To plan or not to plan

Note: This symbol will be used throughout the book wherever observation notes are included.

This is an introductory chapter which outlines the **planning cycle** and introduces two vital concepts: (a) the essential role of observation of children and (b) the fact that respectful and successful learning always starts from the child. Remember to look up the words in bold which you will find explained at the end of each chapter.

The tale of two women

Maria and Julia are both working women. They are both married, have children, live in a city, drive cars and have careers which they value. This is the story of a Monday morning in the life of each one:

> Maria got to bed late on Sunday night. She and her friend Julia had been out to the cinema and she was tired when they got home so she fell into bed without checking her diary, looking online for the weather forecast or preparing for the next day. On Monday morning she got up after the alarm had rung for the second time, put on the clothes she had been wearing the night before, had a bowl of cereal, kissed the children goodbye and set off to get her bus. Once outside she discovered it was much colder than it had been at the weekend: her bare feet in their sandals were freezing and she had

no umbrella, no scarf and no hat. She arrived at work damp, cold and bad-tempered. She was made even more bad-tempered when she realised that she had left the papers she needed for the meeting in her other bag at home.

Julia also got to bed late – even later than Maria, because when she got home from the cinema she quickly checked her diary and made a note of the meeting she needed to be at by ten the next morning. She also looked at her favourite weather website, noted the change in temperature predicted and set out her clothes for the next day. Before she fell into bed she ensured that the notes for her meeting were in her bag – the one she would take with her next day. She arrived at work dry and warm, ready for the coming week and in a good mood.

You may have identified with one or other of those women and we have all certainly had days like Maria's and days like Julia's. What Julia did – quite simply – was that she **planned**. In order to make her morning go well she took several minutes the day before to check that she knew what she was to do on Monday and ensured she had the papers she needed. She checked too that she knew what the weather might bring so that she was prepared in terms of what to wear. Her planning made her morning and her week get off to a good start. There might have been some unplanned-for things to disrupt her plans – the theft of her handbag, for example, or trains not running on time. But apart from things like that, her plan should have allowed her to start the day without undue stress.

Planning is an everyday term – the sort of word which we all use frequently, perhaps without stopping to think what it really means. And we use it in many different contexts and with a range of different meanings. A dictionary definition of the word 'plan' describes it as a scheme or a programme or a method, worked out beforehand, to achieve something, or as a tentative or proposed course of action. Planning then would mean either (a) what one does beforehand in order to achieve a goal or (b) a sequence of actions designed to meet a plan. The great thinker Thoreau said, 'Never look back unless you are planning to go that way.' In effect Julia had a plan. She spent some time the night before, thinking about what she might need to wear and take with her to work based on the information she already held or was able to gather. Maria had no plan.

For professionals involved in the care and learning of babies, toddlers and young children, planning is essential. It is as important as getting dressed in the morning, arriving at work on time and treating the children, their parents and carers and those we work with respectfully. It is only through planning that we can expect to earn respect by being efficient and effective. A number of questions arise from this.

Why plan?

You plan in order to be in control of what you are doing. In terms of your work you plan *for* a number of reasons and *in relation to* a number of different people. This implies that planning carries with it a *focus, roles* and *responsibilities*. As you read through the list that follows, do think about these.

1 You plan to *ensure that the children in your care are looked after, cared for, stimulated appropriately, kept safe, and nourished physically and emotionally*.

- Your responsibilities here are to the children.

- Your focus is on the children.

- The roles you play might include **observing** the children indoors and/or outdoors; setting up the environment; taking notes of what you observe; playing with the children; reading to the children; speaking to them and listening to them; physically caring for the needs of children (changing nappies, feeding babies); talking to parents and carers; and so on.

2 You plan to *ensure that you know what your role will be with the children throughout the day*. You have to plan (either on your own or with your colleagues) which children you will be focusing on; where you will be; what you will be doing. This planning involves thinking about what your role will be throughout the day.

- Your responsibilities here are to the children, even though the focus is on your role.

- The focus will be on what you do.

- Your role may change over the course of the day and it may be determined by the ages of the children and their individual needs.

3   You plan to *ensure that you know what the role of other adults will be.*
    Sometimes the overall planning will have been done by a team leader or
    within a group of professionals. What will be decided is what each
    member will be doing, with which children and where.

    ● Your responsibilities here are to the children and to your colleagues.

    ● Your role might involve you in supporting the work of a colleague
    or in modelling something for others.

4   You plan to *ensure that you know what resources you will need.* When
    you know which children you will be focusing on and where you will
    be, you can plan, with others, what resources you will need.

    ● Your responsibilities are to the children and to your colleagues.

    ● Your role might be to ensure that the resources are suited to the
    interests and needs of these children.

5   You plan to *ensure that parents and carers are kept informed of the
    progress and development of their children.*

    ● Here your responsibilities are to the children and to their parents
    or carers.

    ● Your role is that of informing parents and carers about how well
    their children are doing.

If I asked you, on the basis of what you have just read, to make a plan for
what you might do tomorrow, you would look at me in puzzlement. There
is no way that you – or anyone else – can plan for something unless you
have something to refer to. Essentially, you have to know which child or
children you will be planning for. The key message here is one you will
certainly already know:

You have to start with the child.

You will almost certainly have heard the story of the man who responded to
the question, 'How do I get to London from here?' with the answer, 'Well, if
I were you I wouldn't start from here.' The same is true of asking, 'How do I
plan?' You have to start with the child.

Sue Sheppy (2009) reminds us that when we think of planning for the
personal, social and emotional development of babies in particular we need
to remember that we are the most important resource in the setting. So
planning how we – the teachers and practitioners – will spend our time is

PSED

essential. She says, 'You are the baby's most important resource in the setting. Your time and attention are vital to their well-being and development, and your one-to-one sessions need to be planned for and protected' (Sheppy 2009, p. 22).

I would add that people – adults and children – are the most important resource for all young children if one takes a **sociocultural view of learning** and development. So considering the time and attention of adults, the grouping of children, and the opportunities for sharing and negotiating and discussing, are all essential.

Starting with the child

The Early Years Foundation Stage (EYFS) requires that you plan for the care, learning and development of all the children you encounter in your school or setting who are under the age of six. In essence you may have to plan for babies or toddlers or young children. And it takes little imagination to recognise how different the needs and interests of such a wide range of children will be. Our mantra, **starting with the child**, means all of the following:

- *knowing as much as possible about all the children* for whom you are the key worker;
- *keeping records* about what you know; and
- ensuring that these are shared with and referred to *by all who come into contact with the child.*

This is an ongoing and essential process and is the starting point of the whole planning cycle. The figure on the next page illustrates the process.

1   The first thing you do is to gather **evidence** about the child. You can do this by:
    - *observing* the children at different times, involved in different activities and in different ways;
    - *discussing* the children with parents or carers, or with the previous practitioners, or with colleagues, or often with the child herself;
    - *sharing your findings* with colleagues on a regular basis.

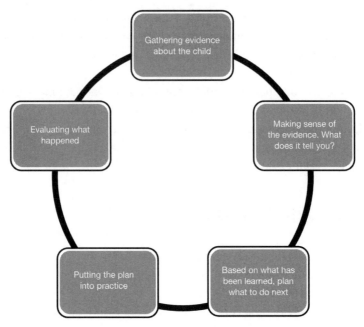

The planning cycle: read it in a clockwise direction, starting at the top

2   Once you have gathered the evidence you need to **assess** it, or make sense of it, and you do this by:

- **recording** what you have found so that it forms a record and is available to others;

- **analysing** the notes you have made in order to tell you about what the child already knows, what the child can already do, what the child is interested in, how the child learns, and what the child's achievements and needs might be;

- *deciding* what it is you think the child needs next in order to take learning and development forward. This gives you the basis for planning.

Steps 1 and 2 relate to the collection of evidence and the interpretation or analysis of this evidence.

3   Armed with the evidence you are ready to plan what to do next. You will see that successful planning really depends on the collection and analysis of the evidence. You might plan all or any of the following:

- Activities matched to the observed interests of the children to allow them to follow their own agendas indoors and out. These activities will offer opportunities for **child-initiated** activities.

- Possible group activities, indoors and out. These would involve an adult and could be described as **adult-initiated** activities.

- What you and the other adults *will actually do*. You may want to think about what roles each adult will play. Who will be observing the children? Who will be playing with the children? Who will be setting up the activity? And so on.

4 Now you put your **plan into practice**. You set up the activities, appropriately resourced, and play the role you have assigned yourself, and ensure that others in your team know what their roles are. This involves ensuring that you and your team:

- **set up and resource** appropriate activities indoors and out;

- *plays the roles allocated* which might include observing particular children, being a play partner, leading a group activity and always being alert to children's interests and needs.

Note: This requires that the planning is either done as a team or shared with all members of the team in a very explicit way.

5 Finally – and most importantly – the **practice is evaluated** (by practice we mean what you planned and evaluated). This is where you think about whether you achieved what you set out to do, and requires that you are able to give evidence for your response. It also requires that you go back to your initial evidence so you can check your planning against that. Here are some questions you can use to check that your planning was appropriate, inclusive and effective:

- Did the planning allow for all children to get **deeply involved** in something? Did someone note which children did get deeply involved and which didn't?

- Was some **challenge** embedded in each activity (child-initiated and/or adult-initiated)?

- Was this challenge **appropriate** to the ages, experience and interests of the children in your group? Give reasons for your response.

- Were the resources used appropriately and **creatively**? Give reasons for your response.

- Did the children use the resources you provided *in ways that were expected or unexpected*?

- Based on this, can you suggest *what the children learned* from this activity?

- Were you able to *play the roles you allocated yourself*? Explain your response.

Now you cannot, of course, do this for every activity throughout the day. You will have to focus on individuals or on groups of children and so will your colleagues, and you need to find time to share your findings so that they become the evidence for the next day's planning. There is much to think about here and you might want to draw breath, think and perhaps read this section again before moving on to our next story – that of Rita and 'her' babies.

The tale of Rita and 'her' babies

Rita has been a nursery school teacher for years. She worked in nursery schools and in nursery classes in schools. This year she decided to change direction, and applied to be and was appointed as a teacher in a children's centre working with the youngest children. In an interview she gave a very clear account of how different an experience this is proving for her:

> I love working with children from aged from three to five. They can talk. They are curious and inventive and responsive and funny and charming and chatty and into everything. Babies seem to be a completely different species. In my first few weeks I thought I would die of boredom. The three babies in our room ate, slept, cried, filled their nappies and once in a while smiled or made some response that I found surprising. I started carrying a novel in my bag, and when the babies were sleeping would sneak time to read. But then a visitor came to see the children's centre and she started to ask me about how I planned. I stared at her in amazement. Planned for what? Making up enough feeds? Changing more nappies? As she was listening to me whine, one of the babies woke up. The visitor went over to the cot and started to talk to the baby. I watched, in amazement, as the baby responded to the voice by making her own sounds. The visitor then shook her head at the baby and the baby

copied this action. I nearly fell over. This was a real **interaction**, with two partners taking turns to contribute to a pattern of response and counter-response. The next day I received, in the post, a note thanking me for having shown her the baby room and inviting me to come and hear a talk she was giving about a recent visit to Reggio Emilia in Italy. I went and it changed my life!

She talked about the system in place in Reggio Emilia where *asili nidi* [the Italian name for the nurseries for children from birth to the age of three and meaning, literally, nests] are provided in many towns and are based on the principle that every child is entitled to quality 'schools'. It is important to note that the word 'school' encompasses group care and education provided for these young children as well as for older children. Theoretically, there should be a seamless transition from these *nidi* to the equivalent of nursery school. She explained that any *nido* involves the active, direct and explicit participation of parents in deciding how the *asilo nido* should operate. In this way this region of Italy provides quality care and education for all children. Before this initiative, only children with special needs were provided for in this way. What makes the *asilo nido* particular and special is the **relationship** between the child and the educator, and the interaction between the family environment and the environment of the *asilo nido* itself. It is a place, essentially, of relationships and communication: it is where a culture of learning and teaching is constructed.

I sat back and thought about that, and continued to think about it over days. What was I doing to create a culture of teaching and learning with my babies? I started to think about these things: how often and how well did I communicate – really communicate – with each baby? And with the baby's parents? I realised I did very little looking, very little listening and very little to suggest I saw each baby as a **competent person**. I started to listen and to look, to talk and to respond, to interact and to make notes. So what do I plan? Well, mainly I plan which baby or babies I might pay particular attention to, although this can always change because the needs of the babies decide how much attention is given. I recognise that for these very young babies the routines of the day dominate – feeding times, nappy changing, sleeping – but that these routines are opportunities for interaction, for looking and listening and the beginning of some of the little rituals of communication. So I talk to the children as I feed them, as I change them and as they begin to go to sleep. I sing to them too and chant little rhymes. I play games with them, using their bodies to introduce them to the possibilities of setting up an interaction between us, or of predicting what will happen next. I might lift up Simeon's feet, count to three and then gently drop them again. This started because I did it once, by chance, and he roared with laughter. Now it has become one of our rituals or games.

I pay close attention to what each of my key children does and make copious notes. I take photographs of the babies when something special happens. I pin up the notes I make and the photographs I take so that parents can come in and read about what their children have done during the day. Here are some of my notes:

Simeon (six months at the start of these notes)

Each note is dated, so that I can see progression. Here the dates have been left out for ease of reading. But the notes are in chronological order.

He passed a rattle from one hand to the other.

When I nodded my head at Simeon he copied my actions and nodded back.

I nodded my head and he copied it, and when I failed to respond he looked intently at me and nodded his head again. This time I copied him and he beamed at me.

Howled with fury, and when I investigated he needed his nappy changing.

Repeated the screaming when his nappy was full – clearly telling me as best he can what he dislikes.

Have had mirrors put over the changing table and Simeon lay there, no nappy on, and beamed at himself in the mirror. Don't think he really knows that it is him.

Observing babies closely and writing down what I notice makes me more aware and focused. On the basis of what I see I may plan something new. For example, the game of dropping his legs went on for several days and then I decided to change it by giving him a kiss on his tummy as I dropped his legs. This greatly amused him and that game continued until he decided to vary it by grabbing my hand and kissing it before I could kiss his tummy.

Rita's story is a fascinating one, charting her own development as an educator and the misconceptions she held when she first started working with babies. The same is often true of those who are trained for or are used to working with children of a particular age and then make a change. The message is clear: all children are potentially competent people and all deserve the highest quality in terms of how they are treated and taught.

What have you learned?

In this chapter we have started to think about what we mean by planning, why it is important to learning and development, how it has to start with what is known about the child at a given point in time and how it forms part of a cycle which is ongoing. Good planning builds on what the child already knows, can do and is interested in, and offers a carefully matched challenge to allow the child to move ahead. You cannot plan if you don't look and listen, take note of what you see and hear, analyse it to find what it tells you about the child and then offer something in terms of resources or interaction or activity to take the learning forward. But how will you know what to offer next unless you have some knowledge of child development? This is where we go in the next chapter.

Note: Key features of learning are in *italic*.

Glossary

adult-initiated: Something which has been started or set up by an adult. Play is not adult-initiated although the adult may have set up the context to stimulate play.

analysing: Examining something carefully in order to understand or explain it.

appropriate: In the context of a challenge, this means that the challenge has been carefully matched to what is known about the child or children in terms of their prior experience, their ages and their interests.

asilo nido (plural: *asili nidi*): The term given to the crèches or nurseries for the youngest children in Italy.

assess: Assessing children's progress is an essential part of your work and you do it both informally and formally, on a daily basis and sometimes to summarise. The Profile (see later) is made up of formative or ongoing assessments but used to summarise achievement.

challenge: Ensuring that activities include something new that makes the child face a problem or think about something. The challenge should never be overwhelming but should be matched to what has been observed about what the child already knows.

child-initiated: This refers to exchanges or experiences which the child has started, and these can be described as play. They are deeply engaging for this very reason.

competent person: Someone who is able to do and understand things. Many researchers and theorists believe we should see all humans, from birth onwards, as competent beings.

creatively: Something that has been done creatively implies that the child has done something in a unique way or produced something new. So the child who solves a problem or produces something never seen before is being creative.

deeply involved: This is when a child is so interested in what she is doing that she spends a long time concentrating on it. *It is a key feature of learning.*

evidence: These are the things you collect which show how the child is learning and developing. They can be your observation notes or photographs, or copies of what the child has made or written, what the child or parent has told you, and so on.

interaction: This means the essential ways in which people relate to and communicate with one another. Many theorists see interaction as *a key feature of good teaching and learning.*

observing/observation: This is what you do on a regular basis as you pay attention to what the children say and do. For the purposes of the EYFS you need to record these in some way – write them down so they become observation notes, date them and keep them to feed into your assessment of learning.

plan: This is where you decide what to do next.

planning cycle: The ongoing process of observing the children, recording your observations, analysing them, planning an activity, setting up the activity and then observing again.

planning into practice: This is what you do when you set up something according to your plan. So what you set up is designed to address the interests and needs you have observed.

practice is evaluated: When you observe what happens in a planned activity you are able to decide whether what you planned met the interests and needs you planned against.

recording: In the context of early learning recording refers to keeping some record of what has been seen and heard by all those involved with a child over a period of time.

relationships: The bonds formed between people. Good and respectful relationships are *essential to successful learning and development.*

set up and resource: This is when you put in place a planned activity or experience together with suitable resources.

sociocultural view of learning: A way of thinking about children and learning in terms of each child's history and culture.

starting with the child: You might be tempted to start with a stepping stone or an early learning goal, but for your observation and planning to make sense you must start with the child. *This is a key feature of planning*

2 Understanding development

Planning for learning 1

When we talk about child development we are not talking about targets or milestones or learning areas or a curriculum. We are talking about what thinkers and researchers have found out about how children, in the social world in which we all live, become able to make sense of the world, to express their thoughts and ideas and feelings and to solve problems they encounter as they themselves raise and answer questions. We take the view of the child as competent being, worthy of respect, and learning, primarily, through language and **communication**. In this chapter we turn our attention to understanding what is thought about how children learn and develop. An understanding of this is essential to planning in the sense that we have to have some theoretical underpinning to analyse what we see and hear, and you now know that it is only by recognising what children already know and can do and are interested in that we can plan for their learning and development.

Key concepts and influences

There is very little room in a book like this to cover in any depth all that is known about how children are thought to develop and to learn best. What we will cover here are some key themes for you to consider and important points to keep in mind as you start on this planning journey. As we discuss these themes we will mention the names of key figures in the field, and if you are interested in their ideas you can easily follow up their work by reading some of the books you will find in the Bibliography.

The table below indicates key concepts regarding what is currently thought about how children develop and learn best and those thinkers, researchers and writers who have thought deeply about these concepts. You will find in the list of influences some names that might be familiar to you and others perhaps not. The key figures are people like Vygotsky and Piaget and you may well have learned something about them. Many of the others have written things that are worth reading, and if you find you have developed a particular interest you might want to follow it up by reading their work.

Key concept	Influences
1 The child as **active learner**: making meaning, curiosity and thinking	Almost all writers and thinkers nowadays agree on this
2 The **social and cultural nature of learning**	Lev Vygotsky, Jerome Bruner, Barbara Rogoff, Judy Dunn, Loris Malaguzzi, Carlina Rinaldi, Colwyn Trevarthen, Iram Siraj-Blatchford et al. (the REPEY project), Gordon Wells, Charmian Kenner, Eve Gregory
3 Relationships and interaction: sustained shared thinking, learning and deep involvement	Lev Vygotsky, Jerome Bruner, Barbara Rogoff, Judy Dunn, Loris Malaguzzi, Carlina Rinaldi, Colwyn Trevarthen, Iram Siraj-Blatchford et al. (the REPEY project), Gordon Wells, Charmian Kenner, Eve Gregory
4 The **physical context of learning** – space, time and resources	Jean Piaget, Elinor Goldschmied, Siraj-Blatchford et al., Malaguzzi and Rinaldi; Margaret Donaldson, Lilian Katz
5 **Enhancing learning** and development: the zone of proximal development, scaffolding and modelling	Vygotsky and Bruner are key figures in this. Also Siraj-Blatchford et al. And all those who adopt a sociocultural stance (see 2)

We look at the first 5 points in this chapter and the remaining 6 in the next chapter.

6 Language and communication	Lev Vygotsky, Jerome Bruner, Barbara Rogoff, Loris Malaguzzi, Carlina Rinaldi, Colwyn Trevarthen, Iram Siraj-Blatchford et al. (the REPEY project), Gordon Wells, Tizard and Hughes
7 The importance of **semiotics**: signs and symbols	Lev Vygotsky, Jerome Bruner, Colwyn Trevarthen, Gordon Wells, Gunther Kress and others
8 **Play** as a mode of learning	Lev Vygotsky, Jerome Bruner, Loris Malaguzzi, Carlina Rinaldi, Iram Siraj-Blatchford et al. (the REPEY project), Colwyn Trevarthen, Gordon Wells, Tina Bruce, Janet Moyles
9 Learning and **schemas**	Jean Piaget, Chris Athey, Cathy Nutbrown, Pat Gura
10 **Questioning** and **theories**	Lev Vygotsky, Loris Malaguzzi, Carlina Rinaldi, Lilian Katz
11 Creativity and feelings: **emotional intelligence**	Loris Malaguzzi and Carlina Rinaldi, Bernadette Duffy, Ferre Laevers, Lilian Katz, Daniel Goleman

The importance of these ideas

1 The child as active learner: making meaning, curiosity and thinking

Today we are used to thinking about children taking charge of their own learning to some extent and we no longer see children as empty vessels waiting to be filled with knowledge, or blank slates waiting to be written on. We know that children are curious, interested, questioning and keen to explore and discover. Perhaps what we don't think about often enough is that this urge to make sense of the world starts from birth (or even before birth) and everything human infants do is designed to **make meaning**. At first exploration is through all their senses and body movements. We now know that the foetus appears to pay attention to sounds before birth, and that babies look and look at the things and people they encounter and respond to differences and changes. We know that babies learn to recognise individual voices of people important in their lives and that the pattern of the human face is significant for them. They make sense of the world of others just as they do of the world of objects. They then move on to making sense of the world of signs and symbols which enables them to communicate through language and other means. Hughes (2009) tells us that:

> What makes us different from all of the animal kingdom is our capacity to think, solve problems and use mental reasoning to plan and work things out. It is our ability to reflect that enables us human beings to be so creative and inventive. White (2002) suggests that there are four characteristics of thinking.
>
> 1 It is intentional.
> 2 It is an activity.
> 3 It employs concepts.
> 4 It is a skill.

I would also like to add that a child needs to be able to think in order to communicate, cooperate and calculate.

Siegler and Alibali (2005: 2) describe thinking in this way:

Thinking obviously involves the higher mental processes: problem solving reasoning, creating, conceptualizing, remembering, classifying, symbolizing, planning and so on. Other examples of thinking involve more basic processes, processes at which even young children are skilled: using language, and perceiving objects and events in the external environment, to name two.

So, where does thinking begin? Maybe the most fundamental aspect of learning is noticing things, that is, making a note in our minds about the presence of something. Tiny babies are making sense of the world through all their senses, and they do this by noticing. What they are noticing is whether the sound they are hearing, the image they are seeing, the touch they are feeling or the scent they are smelling is new or familiar.

Somehow, when you notice something (especially for the first time) whether spontaneously or as a result of it being pointed out, it seems to arouse curiosity and an increased level of attention and interest. Recently I was walking in the woods and noticed an early solitary bluebell in bloom, then found myself looking at the green clumps of sprouting leaves in great detail. The more I looked, the more bluebells I saw! I then found myself examining the flowers and enjoying their exquisite detail.

Curiosity is at the heart of all learning for it leads to active enquiry. What is more, it starts in earnest the day a baby is born. You cannot make someone curious about something, but you can draw their attention to it and help them notice it.

(Hughes 2009, pp. 5–6)

You may have heard of **dispositions**, or habits of mind. They are characteristics or traits that people develop through life and they may be positive or negative and are not fixed. Curiosity is a disposition and it is something that most of us would regard as being positive. After all, an interest in the world and the urge to understand it and the people in it is what prompts us all to find things to read, to explore, to invent and to question. There is evidence that where children's positive dispositions are not appreciated they can become damaged. So nurturing curiosity in children is something we should all be doing.

What to look out for

- Evidence that the child is paying close attention to something, which will suggest that the child is implicitly asking some question. For example, as the child looks at an object, mouths it, shakes it, perhaps she is asking in her head, 'What is this thing? What can I do with it? Does it always stay the same?'

- Evidence that the child is using all means possible in this attempt to make sense of the world – babies using movement and senses, toddlers building a repertoire of exploratory actions and older children making guesses, inventing theories and so on.

- Evidence that the child is beginning or already able to make one thing stand for or represent another. This is a key marker in terms of becoming able to communicate using **symbolic** systems like language.

- Evidence that the child is inquisitive, curious, questioning and exploring.

- Evidence that the child is starting or initiating an exchange with someone.

- Evidence that the child is not only responding to others but often starting exchanges or exploring the world.

The significance of this for planning

- It is only by looking at the children and listening to them that you are able to make an educated guess about what it is they are interested in or paying attention to. So you have to observe closely and make notes as you do. You then need to read through and analyse your notes to see what they tell you about what the child already knows and can do, and also about the child's current interests or passions.

This is the basis for any planning. If you plan something to engage the child you are most likely to enhance learning and development.

2 The social and cultural nature of learning

Many of the theorists and authors on the list are those who adopt a socio-cultural view of learning. This means that they believe that most learning takes place through the interactions that human beings have with one another in the context of home or school or setting or community. Immediately, from birth, the human infant is part of the social and cultural world of the home with its particular language or languages, its customs and arrangements for child-rearing and childcare, its religious and cultural practices, rituals and beliefs. The baby at home is cared for according to the customs of the parents and encounters the language, the touch, the sounds, the smells and the practices of members of the home community. The baby placed in a children's centre or with a childminder or nanny or who goes to a crèche or asilo will experience additional and – to begin with – unfamiliar practices. The baby will have to find a way of enabling the new adults in her life to know what it is she likes or dislikes, fears or needs, enjoys or tolerates. The adult will need to be sensitive to this and to pay close attention to the ways in which each baby begins to communicate. You will remember Rita and the steep learning curve she encountered when she started to conceive of babies as competent learners. You will remember how she started to interact with the babies and talk and sing and chant to them.

Sheppy (2009) reminds us that:

PSED

Babies at this stage are still very much concerned with the basic human needs of food, sleep, warmth and comfort. Bottle-feeding in the setting keeps babies close to a supportive adult to whom they look to provide all their needs and with whom communication is paramount whether it be to signal their need for milk, a clean nappy, a reassuring voice or a nap. Self-care at this stage is unconscious, more of a primal instinct, but gradually, as babies develop, they begin to take an interest in the routines that nourish and sustain them. The signalling becomes more and more refined, the crying increasingly gives way to pointing and to verbal clues. Remember to talk to babies about the routines of the day so that the sounds of the words become familiar to them. As you speak, hold up the object you are referring to, so babies can begin to associate the two. For example, as you get ready to change babies' nappies:

- Name the items: 'Here's your changing mat, let's put it over here. Now where's your clean nappy? Oh, here it is. Can you see the wipes? Oh, they're on the shelf. I will just get some warm water in a little bowl and a cloth to dry your bottom. Now let's have a look. Let's get this wet nappy off. Oh, that's better isn't it? You can have a good kick. We'll soon have you feeling clean and dry again …'

- Make up little repetitive jingles to accompany each stage of the process. 'Here's your mat, mat, mat. How about that, that, that.' Don't worry about what anyone else thinks, this is a one-to-one time for you and the baby to communicate with each other and for them to learn about routines within the setting and start to anticipate what comes next while enjoying the full attention of a supportive adult.

(Sheppy 2009, pp. 128–9)

Vygotsky was the key theorist in adopting a social and cultural approach to learning. He firmly believed that learning – which he saw as the passing on of knowledge from generation to generation – was rooted in interactions between learners and more experienced others who could be either children or adults.

Barbara Rogoff examined the learning of children in cultures other than Western cultures and came to the conclusion that much learning took place through what she called **guided participation**. This term arose out of her observations which showed how much children learned by being alongside more experienced others in their communities. She often talked of this as cognitive apprenticeship. We see it in Western cultures too. Just think of children who watch older siblings engaged in dancing to music, putting on make-up or playing with electronic toys and watch for them re-enacting these behaviours in their play.

What to look out for

- Evidence that children are watching and listening to others, both others of their age and older children and adults. Sheppy (2009) recommends that you ensure that a baby can see what is going on around her. In doing this you enable the youngest children to look

PSED

and listen and learn about the things other children can do, about differences and similarities and about those who make up their community.

- Evidence that children are using others as models by paying close attention to what they do and say.

- Evidence that children mimic the behaviours of others

- Evidence that children are making the sounds and patterns of the languages of their homes.

- Evidence of the ways of relating and forming relationships and learning that they have acquired at home and in their communities.

- Evidence that children are initiating or joining in with social activities – group times, story sessions, singing, mealtimes, ring games, finger plays, games, and so on.

- Evidence that interactions and the roles of adults in your setting are facilitating learning. This means that adults talk to children, listen to them, laugh with them, demonstrate for them, help them, nurture them, respect them, engage with them, pay real attention to them.

The significance of this for planning

- Plan to ensure you have essential information about your key children. You are planning for the overall development and learning for all children in your care. In doing this it is vital that you know as much as possible about the customs and practices and ways of child-rearing and nurturing of each baby in your care.

- Plan to build a culture of respect in your room or setting. Respect for the child's language and culture is essential to building a sound relationship with any child and with the child's parents. Plan how you will demonstrate this to the children and their families and any visitors to your room.

- Plan to provide spaces and time for children to be alone, time to be quiet as well as time to be part of groups and to be noisy.

- Plan how the activities you offer will allow the children to build on their previous experience. This may mean taking a hard look at the resources you provide to ensure that all children will find things that are familiar to them. So, for example, if you have Turkish children in your room, your home corner might include a Turkish coffee pot and some Turkish newspapers and you might invite the woman who works in the local Turkish bakery to come in to demonstrate the making of *gözleme* (stuffed bread).

- Plan for learning through all the interactions and activities in your room. This means you must plan how you will be able to pay attention to how children watch more expert others – either children or adults – and ensure that you make as many opportunities as possible for children to be alongside others throughout the day. You do this when you think in advance about the deployment of adults, groupings of children, and so on.

3 Relationships and interaction: learning, sustained shared thinking and deep involvement

Perhaps you remember that in Rita's story she talked of how, in the *asili nidi* in Reggio Emilia, there is a strong culture of relationships and interaction, and you will not be surprised to learn that for Vygotsky, with his socio-cultural view of learning, relationships and interaction are at the heart of all learning. This, then, is an essential thing to think about in your work with children. Since it is clear that much learning takes place through social interactions, and recent research shows that the best and most successful interactions are those where the more expert other (perhaps the teacher or the parent or the older child or the key worker) shares attention with the learner, this is something you really have to strive to do. Researchers like Colwyn Trevarthen and Jerome Bruner have shown that where mother and child, for example, are in everyday exchanges, the mother and child become able to share the focus of attention. Here are two examples to illustrate this:

Six-month-old Julie looks intently at her doll which is on a shelf in her room. Her mother follows her gaze and gives her the doll.

Nine-month-old Julio points to the apple in the fruit bowl and shakes his head when his grandma hands him the banana.

(Smidt 2006, p. 65)

Sharing the focus of attention with all children is essential and it is not as easy as it sounds. Very often, when your attention is held by a target you are seeking to achieve or a learning goal you have in mind, you don't pay close attention to what it is the child is interested in or focused on. The effect of this is to indicate to the child that you are not 'tuned in' and this makes the child lose interest in whatever it is she is trying to do or find out or express or learn. Recent research from the project Researching Effective Pedagogy in the Early Years (REPEY) showed very clearly that the best outcomes for children were linked to those adult–child interactions that involve what they called **sustained shared thinking**. Here is an example of this cited in the study. Pay close attention to how hard the adult tries to ensure that she and the target child (BOY 1) are focusing on the same thing.

BOY 1 (3.11) hands her a ball of play dough.

NNEB 1: I wonder what is inside? I'll unwrap it.
NNEB 1 [*quickly makes the ball into a thumb pot and holds it out to BOY 1*]: It's empty.
BOY 1 [*takes a pinch of play dough and drops it into the thumb pot*]: It's an egg.
NNEB 1 [*picking it out gingerly*]: It's a strange shape.

Another child tries to take the 'egg'.

To BOY 1: What's it going to hatch into?
BOY 1: A lion.
NNEB 1: A lion? ... Oh, I can see why it might hatch into a lion, it's got little hairy bits on it.

NNEB 1 sends BOY 1 to put the egg somewhere safe to hatch. He takes the egg and goes into the bathroom. After a few minutes BOY 1 returns to the group.

NNEB 1: Has the egg hatched?
BOY 1: Yes.

NNEB 1: What was it?

BOY 1: A bird.

NNEB 1: A bird. We'll have to take it outside at playtime and put it in a tree so it can fly away.

(Siraj-Blatchford et al. 2002, Document 421, Vignette 8)

At no point in this example does the adult suggest that the child is being foolish or unrealistic. She joins in with the child's fantasy, and in doing this she allows the child to pursue his interests. She shows respect for his thinking and his struggle. Now this is very important and it links to the findings of Ferre Laevers, who showed that, where children become deeply involved in what they are doing, significant and high-level thinking is taking place and it is clear that children are learning. Being deeply involved means being able to spend a lot of time concentrating on some issue that is of interest to the child.

What to look out for

- Evidence that in your daily practice you are making every effort to know what it is that children are paying attention to and that you are focusing on this. This means you avoid asking empty questions to which you have an answer you expect to receive. An example of an empty question is to ask the child who is pretending to cook, 'How many have you got in the pan?' when the answer is both obvious to you and of no relevance to the child.

- Evidence that interactions between you and the children are meaningful and serious.

- Evidence that the other members of your staff team are similarly engaged with the children.

- Evidence that children are deeply involved in the activities you provide. You can assess this by observing how hard a child is concentrating and how long the child spends on the task

The significance of this for planning

- If you are to offer activities to involve children, you have to know what the children in your groups are interested in. You cannot, of course, plan an individual programme for each child. But you can pay attention, and when you spot an interest you can set up an activity and see who joins in and how deeply engaged they are.

Meera noticed that two children were busy playing with shoes. They took theirs off and swapped them and then put on one another's. They compared them, and so on. She decided to make a shoe shop in a corner of the room and set it up with empty shoe boxes and pairs of shoes – sandals, slippers, trainers, high-heeled shoes, ballet shoes, football boots, and so on. She borrowed a foot measure from her local shoe shop and wrote labels and price tags. Remember that she had planned this in response to the observed interest of two children. She noticed that over the weeks all the children played in there and the play involved many aspects of learning. She regarded it as one of the most successful activities set up that term.

- In your planning you should ensure that you don't split the day up into short periods of time or change activities too often. Allow children to spend as much time as they need and to follow things through to a conclusion that satisfies them.

William negotiated with the headteacher that the children in the nursery class should not be asked to join in with assemblies or have to go into the hall for PE. He then talked to his fellow workers about having long stretches of time during which children could get deeply involved in something or move through a series of activities, trying them out until they found something to engage them.

- If you are really planning to engage children and allow them to explore, in depth and over time, you have to plan to pass on control to the children for much of the time. This means that you will plan activities which are based on the observed interests of the children and which are open-ended enough to allow the children to follow through what interests or concerns them. This also means you plan a largely child-initiated curriculum where adults are carefully deployed to interact and to observe.

Archana and her fellow workers plan carefully what activities they will set out each week. They are determined that activities will remain largely the same over time, allowing the children to follow up their interests. Changes that are made are small changes, built on what the staff have observed has been happening. For example, in the water tray, when the children seemed to be getting stuck in their play, they added a collection of objects with holes of different sizes and laid out in different ways and patterns. This allowed the children's play and thinking to be challenged as the children noticed what happened when there were many holes rather than one, a large hole as opposed to a small one, and so on. This is planning using the **theory of 'Match'**.

- In terms of planning adult-initiated activities you will want to plan story sessions, outings, singing or music-making activities, and you will want to plan in terms of the size of groups, the ages and needs of the children, and the support offered in terms of ensuring all the children in the group have access to the activity. In this we are thinking about providing story props to draw speakers of languages other than English into the stories, visual support for those with visual difficulties, and so on.

Tahiba leads a team of workers and they meet for a brief and targeted session at the end of each day. This meeting reviews what happened that day and is mainly about planning adult-initiated activities for the next day. So the responses of children are discussed and then each worker volunteers to run a story session or a music session, take children on a local outing, or perhaps run a book-making session. This is for groups of three- to five-year-olds. The policy allows children to choose where to go for most of the day, but this planning session might suggest that particular children be invited to go with a particular adult for an activity planned to meet their observed needs.

4 The physical context: space, time and resources

Piaget was the researcher who influenced many educationalists in the 1960s. He believed that the role of the adult educator was to provide a stimulating environment, rich in learning opportunities. This is something we now all take for granted. In almost any setting for young children in the developed world, you will find home corners with miniature versions of what is available in the adult world – small cookers and beds and tables and chairs and Hoovers and washing machines, and so on. You will find building blocks and construction toys and train tracks and bikes and trikes and climbing frames and toys and games and dolls and everything else that we believe young children need in order to learn. In essence, we provide environments for budding consumers. It is important to remember that children who don't have access to all of this learn just as well as those who do.

Stella Louis, in her book for this series called *Knowledge and Understanding of the World*, reminds us that we live in a highly technological world, and this is true for those of us in the developed world, having access to computers and machines and programmable toys. But we need to remember that children not having access to these things still learn, and even if we turn our attention to learning about ICT we need to remember that it is about ways of communicating, and about language and symbols. It is a way of finding and solving problems, and what we need to be alert to is just how children – even very young children – set about asking questions, seeking solutions and arriving at their own theories.

So although resources are important – certainly books are – they do not, in themselves, ensure that children will learn and develop. In Japanese nurseries children have access primarily to more open-ended materials – cardboard boxes and lengths of fabric. In some of the German nurseries children are taken out, every day, into the woods where their resources are the trees and the seeds and the sticks and the stones they find. In the famous *asili* in Reggio Emilia the rooms for the youngest children have mirrors everywhere – on ceiling and floor, inside cubes, at child height. This is to help these babies learn that they are unique and separate from others, but part of a community. In all the nursery provision in that region space is regarded as an essential ingredient in learning, and each *asilo* has a *piazza* or square mirroring the squares found in all towns and cities, which are places where people meet and talk and build their communities. In some of the nurseries there are studios or ateliers where beautiful things are gathered together, with paints and clay and other creative material on offer and sometimes with an artist in residence working there, modelling how ideas and feelings can be represented.

Nurse (2009) talks of the importance of space with regard to physical development in particular. She suggests that practitioners critically review the space available indoors and out and maximise what is usable by young

KUW

PD

children by removing things like tables and chairs (pp. 58–9). She advocates the use of what are called 'movement corners', which are places where activities are set out or offered on the floor rather than on a table and where children can find ways of playing or listening or talking which are physically comfortable for them.

You may well have come across the ideas of Elinor Goldschmied, who studied the development of infants and said that they needed to be able to spend prolonged periods of time exploring natural objects like pine cones and corks. This led to the development of the ever popular treasure baskets. Anita Hughes, in her book *Problem Solving, Reasoning and Numeracy* (2009), worked with Goldschmied, and she tells us that:

> The most significant things about **heuristic play** are that it is self-chosen, experimental and non-social. Non-social means that children play with the material because they are interested in how that material can be manipulated. Children may copy an adult or another child. However, the play demands concentration and focus, which social interaction with others would interrupt. It is therefore very important for the adult to sit nearby (having set out a range of materials attractively) and be responsive but not intrusive. Indeed, it is best to stay quiet and simply be peaceful and comfortable to allow a small group of children to concentrate without the fear of interruption or distraction.
>
> Some typical behaviour that can be described as heuristic play is as follows:

- picking up objects and putting them in different places;
- putting objects in containers such as tins, boxes, tubes and trolleys;
- emptying objects out of containers;
- piling objects into towers and knocking them down;
- rolling objects along the floor;
- sliding objects through tubes or down sloping surfaces;
- slotting small objects inside larger objects;
- lining up objects;

PSRN

- shaking or banging objects together;

- collecting similar or identical objects and putting them in containers or in heaps;

- putting rings on rods, posts, handlebars, etc.;

- spinning cylindrical or round-shaped objects;

- dropping objects from a height;

- screwing or unscrewing lids;

- squeezing objects in fists or between fingers and thumb;

- looking inside or through objects;

- draping ribbons, scarves and chains around their necks.

(Hughes 2009, p. 29)

Goldschmied believed that time with the objects should be silent, with no adult intervention. This flies in the face of the evidence that all learning is social, so you will have to decide for yourselves whether you plan to intervene or to stay silent.

In our nursery provision we are concerned that children should have access to learning all day, indoors and out, and the importance of outdoors is that it allows for exploration on a different scale. There is more room to run and jump and climb and construct. Activities relating to building and transporting and rotation and enclosure can all be offered on a much larger scale. Nurse (2009) points out that requirements for settings to offer some outdoor space vary enormously from area to area and have, in fact, been watered down so that the words 'must provide outdoor play space' have been replaced with 'should' in recognition of the fact that the provision of onsite outdoor space is often not possible. This is an issue being faced by many state providers and those in the private and voluntary sectors. In terms of meeting the overall learning needs of children this is a significant issue.

Margaret Donaldson, aware of the fact that children entering formal schooling struggled to cope with abstract concepts, began to examine the reason for this, and she found that children needed experience of real things which they could physically explore before being able to deal with more abstract things. She developed the concept of **meaningful contexts**, and what she meant by this was things and activities whose purpose was clear to these young children. She believed – as I do – that asking children to do

PD

something like complete a worksheet where they are required to colour all the big balls blue and all the little balls green, or to collect objects starting with the letter 'r' into a set, is trivial and meaningless. The child can see no reason or purpose for these activities – and there is, indeed, no sensible reason for them. In Donaldson's words, activities like this do not make **human sense** to children. But cutting sandwiches in half, buttering bread, planting seeds, setting the table, pretending to shop, threading beads to make a necklace, bathing the dolls, are all activities whose purpose is clear. Through much experience like this children become able to move from **everyday concepts** and activities to more abstract ideas, or what Vygotsky called **scientific concepts**.

What to look out for

- Evidence that the space available is well used.

- Evidence that the existing arrangement of activities and furniture allows the children to move freely and easily and access what they need.

- Evidence that the resources offered allow the children to find and use what they need without unnecessary difficulties. You are looking to see that pairs of scissors cut, pencils are sharpened, pens have not dried out, and so on.

- Evidence that the resources are engaging children in fulfilling and satisfying exploration and expression, and if they are not, making the necessary changes.

- Evidence that children are starting to use one thing to stand for or represent another. They might put a plastic cup on their heads as a hat or use a block of wood as a telephone. This is a significant moment in learning and is significant precisely because the ability to do this enables children to deal with all the communicative systems we have which are symbolic – reading, writing, number, and so on.

- Evidence that the activities make human sense to the children. Do they allow the children to draw on their previous experience? Do they allow the children to have first-hand or direct experience of exploring aspects of the world?

- Evidence of any children displaying repeated patterns of behaviour – exploring what happens when you transport things from one place to another, or when you cover things up, or when you move yourself or objects round and round. This is an indication of schemas, which we will look at later.

- Evidence that the resources you offer are cared for, complete, clean, attractive, easily accessible and safe. As we have said before, pairs of scissors should cut; clay should not be dried out; puzzles must be complete.

The significance of this for planning

- Plan your resources and your space, indoors and out, considering scale and purpose.

- Review and plan or alter areas of your room to allow children to have space to move easily and to work alongside or with others.

- Plan how you can provide secret or hidden places for children where they can go with a toy or a book or another child.

- Plan how resources will be checked and maintained.

- Plan for activities outdoors which will continue to meet observed needs on a larger scale than indoors.

- Plan activities which will make human sense to the children, allow them to draw on their previous experience and allow them to have first-hand or hands-on experiences.

- Consider carefully what resources to offer in relation to the activities you set out to meet the observed interests of children. If, for example, you are setting up a garden centre because you have noticed one or two children digging in the garden, think about the possibilities for writing in that area. Think about picture or story books which are related to gardens and which you can make available or read to the children.

5 Enhancing learning: the zone of proximal development, scaffolding and modelling

It was Vygotsky who drew attention to the fact that what we see children doing as they complete tasks that we have given them is only an indication of how they are performing at one point in time. It does not tell us what they are capable of. This led to the development of his now-famous zone of proximal development (or ZPD) which was the notional gap between what the child can do alone and what the child might do with help. This is a very important idea and one which has continued to be developed by followers of Vygotsky. In essence, what he was saying was that a more expert learner (who could be a parent, a teacher or practitioner or another child), who is tuned in to what the child is doing (back to shared attention), can help the child take the next step in learning by giving physical or verbal help. Bruner gave this help the name **scaffolding**, which uses the analogy of the physical scaffold put up against a building to allow improvements or changes to be made. When the work is complete the scaffold is removed. When the help has been given, the learner can do something independently without needing the help.

Here is an example of an adult scaffolding a child's learning, drawn from a small observation made by Susan Bragg (Smidt 1998):

> Louisa was involved in making things at the 'making table'. She started off with a plan she had drawn and then went in search of the resources she had decided she needed.
>
> ... as she walked over to the wood she said to herself, 'Now what bit do I need?' Taking a long piece of wood in her other hand she returned to her seat. She placed the wood on the table, saying, 'This is big enough,' and then emptied the beads out of her hand onto the table. Next she took the glue and squeezed little blobs of it along the wood ...
>
> She carried on in this way, talking the process aloud and showing her work in progress to the other children. Then she needed something to stick two pieces of wood together. First she remembered the glue gun and asked the adult to help her with that. But it didn't work. Then she decided to attach some foam to a piece of wood, but the glue gun did not work on that either. Noticing that Louisa was getting frustrated the adult suggested using an elastic band.

'Good. It worked!' she said, looking at the other children. 'That's good, isn't it, using an elastic band?'

(Bragg, in Smidt 1998, pp. 143–5)

The consequence of that small but focused intervention was to allow Louisa to work for 45 minutes to make her 'boat' and fulfil her plans. This child was deeply involved in what she was doing. The adult took careful note of what she was doing and recognised when she reached an insurmountable obstacle. This allowed the adult to intervene and scaffold Louisa's learning.

Adults working with very young children are very often in the role of **modelling**. They are the most obvious 'expert other' and often they show children what is expected in terms of behaviour, or model for them how 'experts' do things. Every time you speak to a child you provide a model of effective spoken language. Every time you read a story you show how readers read. Every time you do anything that the infant or child cannot yet do you provide a model for how it should or could be done.

What to look for

- Evidence that what you and your colleagues are doing in terms of observing children in order to identify their interests and concerns is enabling you to both share attention with them and scaffold their learning.

- Evidence that when you scaffold learning you offer both verbal and physical help.

- Evidence that you praise children appropriately in the sense of really focusing on what the child has done rather than giving meaningless praise like 'Lovely' or 'Good boy'.

There is a now-famous story of four-year-old Nicola being asked to look after a little girl new to the nursery class. Nicola helped the new child put on a painting apron and the two little girls painted side by side. Then the new child unclipped her painting from the easel and set off across the room. Nicola stopped her to ask, 'What are you doing?' The new child said, 'I going to show the teacher' Nicola's response to this was to say, 'Oh, don't bother. She will just tell you it is beautiful.' Think about this!

- Evidence that you model what readers do. Or writers. Or speakers. Or listeners. Or efficient users of scissors or pencils or forks or knives.

- Evidence that you model respectful behaviour. Or enjoyment of the company of others. Or how to share. Or to trust.

The significance of this for planning

- This is a difficult area to plan for because your responses to what you observe will determine how you behave. If you see a child who needs physical help you will give that, and you will almost certainly always praise children's efforts. What you can plan to do is to ensure that your praise will be targeted and meaningful, and not empty.

- You might also want to plan a morning where you observe a colleague to watch how she models things for the children and how she scaffolds their learning, and then invite this colleague to do the same for you.

What you have learned

In this chapter we have started to look at some of the key concepts in terms of human development and in terms of effective teaching. We have thought about how children, from birth, actively seek to understand the world and everything in it. We have thought about the importance of interactions with others and about the physical contexts for learning. We have paid attention to what adults can do to set up activities which have a clear purpose that is evident and meaningful to children, how they can embed matched challenges into the activities on offer and how, by sharing the focus of attention with children, they can help them get deeply involved in an activity. We carry this on in the next chapter. So do read on.

Glossary

active learner: This means a learner who is not passive but actively seeks to understand and explain the world. Piaget and Vygotsky were among the first thinkers to see human infants like this.

communication: The ways in which humans share meanings and ideas. One of the primary, but not the only means of communication is language. *Essential for learning*.

dispositions: These are ways of behaving or habits of mind which might be either positive or negative.

emotional intelligence: We are used to thinking about intelligence in terms of thinking about the physical world; emotional intelligence refers to thinking about the world of feelings and of others.

enhancing learning: What practitioners and others can do to help children take the next step in learning. It means, literally, to make learning better.

everyday concepts: These are the concepts that children come to understand through their direct and hands-on explorations of objects and activities

guided participation: A term used by Barbara Rogoff to describe how children learn through being engaged with adults or more expert learners in the activities relating to their lives. This is sometimes referred to as cognitive apprenticeship.

heuristic play: The play where babies explore the physical properties of objects.

human sense: Young children, in order to learn effectively, need to be able to see the purpose or point of what they are doing.

making meaning: This is what we all do when we try to make sense or to understand anything we encounter. Children are meaning-makers from birth.

meaningful contexts: The term used by Donaldson to refer to activities whose purpose is clear to the learners.

modelling: What we all do, which is to show children how experts do things like talk, walk, read, write, skip, smile, praise and so on.

physical context of learning: Where the learning takes place, this refers to the space (indoors or out, and so on), the materials or resources used, the tools offered, and so on.

play: An over-used and often not clearly understood term. It means what children do when they choose what and how to do something. If you tell a child to go and play, the child is following an adult instruction and is not in control.

questioning: There is much evidence that from birth human infants seek to make sense of the world, and they do this through exploration and asking implicit (not spoken or heard) questions. *Questioning is an essential learning tool.*

scaffolding: A term first used by Bruner to describe what others (children or adult) can do to help children move from being dependent on help to being able to do something independently – i.e. to bridge the zone of proximal development.

schemas: Repeated patterns of action showing how some children follow a theme or an interest in as many ways and contexts as possible.

scientific concepts: Another way of describing concepts which are abstract. It takes young children time to arrive at these, and they arrive at them through using direct experience and first developing everyday concepts.

semiotics: The study of the system of signs or symbols built up by different cultures. Since most school learning involves signs and symbols, *coming to understand these is essential.*

social and cultural nature of learning: Vygotsky and many others believe that all learning comes about through the passing on of knowledge and hence is bound to both society and culture.

sustained shared thinking: Where the learners and others (child or adult) are focused on the same thing. *Essential feature of successful learning and teaching.*

symbolic: Where one thing stands for or represents another. Important for school learning because many of our cultural tools are symbolic. Reading and writing depend on letters and words which are symbols, and so on. You will find a fuller explanation in the next chapter.

theories: The explanations that children make up for things that interest them and that they want to explain.

theory of 'Match': This is where practitioners make a small change to an activity in response to what they have observed about how the children respond to the activity. The change is neither too small (hence no challenge) nor too big (danger of failure), but matched to the observed needs of the child.

3

Understanding development

Planning for learning 2

In this chapter we continue our exploration of key concepts in terms of development and planning. We have considered the importance of the physical environment and the sociocultural nature of learning, and have examined interaction and looked at ways of extending learning. We now turn our attention to other key concepts.

6   Language and communication

All the theorists who have been described as adopting a **sociocultural stance** are deeply interested in the importance of language and communication in learning and development. We find here the ideas of Vygotsky and Bruner, also the thoughts of Malaguzzi and Rinaldi from Reggio Emilia, the findings of those involved in the REPEY project and the work of Colwyn Trevarthen and Gordon Wells with babies around language. You will know that it is through interactions with others that human infants begin to develop language skills. We know that the newborn infant is attuned to the sound of the mother's voice, and much has been written about how the human infant not only responds to communication with others but often initiates it. Rod Parker-Rees (2007) has written much about early communication and talks of familiarity as being the basis of both joint attention and playfulness. Some may find the tone of this work rather sentimental but there is little doubt that the nature of the relationship between the partners in any communicative exchange will affect the very nature of that exchange. Sroufe and Wunsch (1972) showed that the actions most likely to make a child smile are those performed by a parent and those most likely to make a child cry are those performed by a stranger. For those of us working with young children it is important to remember how vital caring, respectful and nurturing relationships will be.

Vygotsky and Bruner both regarded language as essential to learning. Bruner's early work related to the role played by adults in helping children acquire language and in his work he looked at things other than talk – things like **eye-pointing**, pointing, body language, gesture, inflection, signs and intonation. He was the first person to look into the importance of turn-taking games and routines in the lives of babies (things like playing 'peeka-boo' and predictive games) and he drew attention to how human infants play with language (the sounds and the rules) just as they play with objects. This playfulness with language was something he regarded as very sig-nificant. We can support and extend this delight in playing with language through the rhymes we chant, the songs we sing, the stories we read or tell and the games we invent around letters and sounds and words. In the best practice, care is taken to greet or count or sing or tell or read stories in the languages of the group. This may require the support of older children, adult speakers of the languages or community leaders.

Vygotsky was interested in the links between thought and language. He looked at how children sometimes use spoken language in order to talk themselves through a process. This is known as **monologuing** and you may heard children in your care using this. Even when this is not apparent Vygotsky believed that children use spoken language internally (and he called it inner speech) and once it is no longer spoken aloud it has become thought. This is a gross over-simplification so if you are very interested in this do read more widely.

In all homes the lives of children are bathed in language, and all lan-guage and languages are equally efficient for thinking and problem solving. Tizard and Hughes and Gordon Wells all carried out longitudinal studies to examine this and all found the same things. When speaker and listener are equal partners in an exchange, language facilitates learning. Sometimes, when children start school, the adults fail to structure meaningful exchanges and end up asking children meaningless questions of no interest or rele-vance to the child, or they ask **closed questions**. Closed questions, which require only a 'yes' or 'no' response, do not create dialogue or enhance learning. You will remember that the REPEY project emphasised the impor-tance of any questioning done by educators being based on shared attention and a desire to communicate rather than to test.

We have already spoken about scaffolding, and how the supportive steps children are helped to take as they move from dependence on help to independence can be in the form of physical help or verbal help. You might want to think very carefully here about what you feel about Goldschmied's idea that babies exploring objects (through treasure baskets) should do this without any verbal interaction from others.

The whole area of language and learning is a complex and a fascinating one and one that we don't have space to explore in any detail here. For Vygotsky, language was seen as a **cultural or psychological tool** and was essential to learning. (It is important to note that language is certainly not just English and not even only spoken or written languages: rather, it refers to any organised and rule-bound system which allows for communication.) So when Loris Malaguzzi said that young children have **a hundred languages** he meant that they should have access to many different ways of expressing and sharing their ideas and feelings. Languages can then mean drawing and painting and making and mathematics and dance and drama and music and much more.

Practitioners involved in the EYFS are involved in identifying and supporting children's earliest attempts at making sense of the world of symbols and signs, which means that they are involved in helping children come to understand the worlds of reading and writing. Helen Bradford, in her book in this series *Communication, Language and Literacy*, reminds us that children are engaged in attempting to join the community of sign/symbol users when she talks about emergent literacy:

> Emergent literacy establishes the fact that children will already be experimenting with mark-making and writing from a very early age, before they begin to use the alphabetic principle of letter–sound relationships and despite the fact that the writing produced might not be conventional from the perspective of an adult. Studies spanning a twenty-year period can be found to support this line of thinking. Harste et al. (1984) discovered that children as young as three were already making planned organisational decisions about their writing and that they wrote with an expectation that the marks they made would make sense, a characteristic of the writing process termed 'intentionality'. Many three-year-olds, for example, have developed a mark which to them represents their name. Goodman (1986) argued that children from the age of two engage

CLL

in writing tasks for a wide variety of reasons and that most have begun to use symbols to represent real things. Lancaster (2003) found that before the age of two children are already able to distinguish between writing, drawing and number. This is based on the child's experience and perceptions of how each of these three domains individually represents meaning. Universal patterns of behaviour reflecting a common set of cognitive processing decisions on the part of children have been identified, such as children making marks that reflect the written language of their culture when asked to write. Such research is important because it suggests that the marks children make on paper are deliberate and purposeful instead of being unorganised and random as they might appear to an inexperienced onlooker.

(Bradford 2009, pp. 22–3)

What to look out for

- Evidence that children are both experiencing and using the languages of both their homes and the setting. Check that you know what languages are heard and spoken by the children in your care. You need to know this so that you are in a position to recognise the sounds and the shapes of the letters in these languages in the children's verbalising or mark-making.

- Evidence that children are initiating exchanges or turn-taking rituals. Collect this evidence.

- Evidence of children's playfulness in using language. Collect this evidence.

- Evidence that you and your colleagues base your questioning of children on shared attention and as part of a genuine dialogue.

- Evidence of children's use of spoken language, moving from babbling to their first words, to sentences and eventually to the complex verbal skills required to communicate verbally. Collect the evidence.

- Evidence that all routines (feeding times, nappy changing, and so on) are bathed in spoken language or song or rhyme.

- Evidence of children using early monologues. Collect this evidence.

- Evidence of a language-rich environment. Do you ensure that you tell and read stories and rhymes and sing songs and engage in finger plays and predictive verbal games throughout each and every day?

- Evidence of a young child asking (with or without words) a question to try and understand the world. Keep this evidence.

The implications for planning

- You will certainly want to ensure that when you plan what to offer and what the adults will be doing, you emphasise the importance of spoken language in enhancing learning. This could be through the songs and rhymes and stories and games you introduce or through your responses to individual children and children in groups. Language – when it is targeted and focused – is an extremely potent tool and one you should try and refine. You are seeking to plan and deliver a language-rich curriculum. Do remember that stories read or told in English need to be supported by visual cues to draw in those having first languages other than English.

- Arrange to visit another practitioner with a view to listening to how she uses language in interaction with the children. Take notes. Then invite the practitioner to do the same for you. Try and see if you dominate or if you are as good at listening as you are at talking. Remember that both are essential to dialogue, and dialogue is essential to enhancing learning.

- Try and see if you make unfocused comments like 'Well done!' or 'Good' or 'Very nice' or if you genuinely notice what the child is paying attention to and comment on that. This is a skill you need to develop!

- You must plan all adult-initiated activities and think carefully about which children they are targeted at, what the role of the adults will be and what the purpose of the activity is. So you have to plan which stories to tell or read to which children, which children to take on small local outings (to the park or the shops or round the neighbourhood, and so on). Alternatively you can choose which story to read or which game to play and allow the children to choose to attend or not.

7 The importance of semiotics: signs and symbols

You will know that young children, in their play, begin to use one thing to represent or stand for another. This means that the children are beginning to be able to use a symbol – something that represents something else. You will know that our spoken language is symbolic: the word 'dinosaur' stands for huge prehistoric creatures. Our written language is symbolic: the letters that make up the word 'dinosaur' are also symbols. Our number system is symbolic: the digit 5 stands for one more than 4 and one fewer than 6. We have a system of musical notation that is symbolic. We use symbols to represent actions: the sign + means put two or more things together. We all recognise the symbol for danger or for bus stop, or for tube station or for the congestion charge zone. And so on.

For Vygotsky the ability to use symbols was very significant and for him it marked the point at which children start being able to make use of events that have happened previously. A child who uses a stick to be a horse has to have some experience or knowledge of what a horse is and what a horse does in order to do this. So when the child uses the stick as a horse, the child does not need to have a real horse present in order to recall something about a horse. Rather, the memory of the horse prompts the child to use the stick as a horse. Abstract learning requires the memory of real experiences or objects.

You will have seen children using things to represent other things and you should pay attention to this because it represents a significant leap in learning. And becoming able to use semiotics – systems of signs and symbols – is essential to being able to learn to read and write, talk, build, draw, count, measure and communicate your ideas.

What to look out for

● Evidence of children using one thing to represent another.

Colin used a ball to be a baby and a mop bucket to be the baby's pram. He sustained this play over several hours and involved other children and adults in his symbolic play, as when he insisted on leaving 'the baby' in the shade when he went inside to have his dinner.

● Evidence of children beginning to incorporate symbols or signs into their play – as when children start making marks on paper as in Zac's writing below:

The first piece of 'writing' presented to his mother by Zac.

The significance of this for planning

- Plan to provide materials which can be used in different ways. A toy Hoover is not very open-ended, but lengths of fabric, empty containers, wooden blocks and materials like these allow children to use them as they choose. They also allow children to choose for themselves what the materials can represent. Helping children do this is really important.

- Plan to offer graphic materials in all activities, indoors and out. This invites children to make up their own marks as they explore their ideas of what it is that people do when they make marks.

- Plan to model mark-making for the older children, as when you scribe a song or a story in large book format or when you write a list of names in a register or a note to parents. Make this visible to the children.

- Plan to model what expert readers do when you read aloud to children. Make the actions of following text, turning pages and examining pictures explicit.

- Plan to collect examples or samples of the marks children make. Keeping these provides you with a very graphic, detailed and personal record of progress in this important area of learning.

8 Play as a mode of learning

Nowadays it is fashionable to talk about play as 'children's work', and while this may be true it is often said by people who don't understand what makes play something particular or why it is important as a way of learning. In some cultures play is regarded as something trivial and something that has no place in learning. Those of us involved in working with young children have a responsibility to be able to explain to parents and others just what it is that makes play a particular and important way of learning, even though it is not the only **mode of learning**.

What makes play unique is that it is under the control of the child. It is what the child chooses to do, together with how to do it, when to do it, when to stop and when to change direction. This means that play is risk-free, because if the child doesn't achieve what she set out to do, she can change direction. Because the child has chosen to do something, we can assume that what the child is doing is of interest to her and that she will be deeply engaged in it. In her play she can bring together many of her developing ideas and concerns, and it is this aspect of play that has allowed some people like Tina Bruce to describe play as an **integrating mechanism**. Vygotsky was particularly interested in **symbolic play** and in **role play** or **pretend play**, and he saw each of these as ways in which children developed rules, negotiated rules with other players, adapted rules to meet changing circumstances and were able to create and manage complex and intricate **play scripts**.

Here are some examples:

> Helen plays at being the manager of a canteen. She chose to wear a paper cap and an apron she found in the home corner and she also went to fetch the 'open and shut' sign which was used in the shop. She stood with her hands on her hips, ordering people around and being very obviously busy.
>
> Donald and Gerit are on the climbing frame. Donald shouts out a warning that there are crocodiles in the water below. Gerit immediately accepts this scenario and arms himself with special weapons that he calls pistols to keep the two safe from the crocodiles. The two are negotiating and changing the play script and the play continues over most of the morning.

In play, children can try out how it feels to be the baby or the mother, the teacher or the learner, the doctor or the patient, the strong or the weak. The child can explore issues of serious concern and interest – death and love and fear and jealousy. Play is a way of learning and one in which Vygotsky believed a child behaved as though he were 'a head taller than himself' (Vygotsky 1967, p. 16). In play children often use one thing to stand for another (a stick becomes a horse, a magic wand, a writing implement). In the developed world, play has become something highly prized. This is apparent in the EYFS Statutory Framework, which states that 'All areas [of learning and development] must be delivered through planned play, with a balance of adult-led and child-initiated activities' (DfES 2007a, p. 11). For me this is a confusing statement because for me play is self-chosen. Adults can, of course, set up and offer a range of interesting, serious and relevant activities to stimulate play, but ultimately it is only when the child has chosen what to do, how to do it and with whom that we can legitimately call it play. And we do need to remember that children do learn not only through play but also through listening to stories, watching things on screens, going to the shops, walking round the garden, talking to their peers at lunchtime – in fact, learning takes place all the time.

What to look out for

- Evidence of children following their own concerns and interests and getting deeply involved in this.

- Evidence of children making up rules to organise their play and noticing when and how they adapt or change these.

- Evidence of children playing roles as they play.

- Evidence of children using symbols in their play.

- Evidence of children revealing their feelings through their play.

- Evidence of children sometimes playing alone, sometimes in parallel or sometimes in co-operation.

- Evidence of some of the questions children seem to be attempting to answer through their play.

- Evidence of children's emotional development through the demonstration of a **range of affect** in play. You are looking to see children who are sometimes happy and sometimes not, sometimes in charge and sometimes following.

- Evidence of infants using their bodies and their senses as they explore objects.

- Evidence of children implicitly asking, 'What is this? What does it do? What can I do with it?'

- Evidence of children using monologue and/or inner speech and/or social speech in play.

The implications for planning

- Check that the activities you are planning are in accord with what you and your colleagues have observed to be the interests of some of the children.

- Plan for there to be familiar things in the activities, to allow children to draw on previous experience.

- Check that there is a challenge embedded in the activities to enhance the learning of some children.

- What role do you plan to take in the activities? And your colleagues?

- Have you planned for at least one adult to be taking notes in order to feed back to you about the effectiveness of your planning and to help you plan further?

- Have you planned what resources you will need? Have you thought about how these will facilitate the play? Have you checked that the resources are in good order?

9 Learning and schemas

You will almost certainly have come across young children who present you (and often their parents and carers) with behaviour that is baffling and irritating and seemingly random:

> In the day-care setting that Val and her friend Suzy attend there is a well-stocked role-play area. The friends are both just over two years old. At the moment, the role-play area is set up to be used as a café, with tables, chairs, plates, tablecloths, cutlery and menu cards for children to choose what they would like to order. Each day recently, Val and Suzy have come to play in the café, bringing with them their dolls and buggies. To the practitioners' dismay, they have packed up the entire contents of the café into their buggies and wheeled them to the book area where they have carefully unpacked all the café equipment and have laid out the tablecloth and cutlery on the carpet in the book area. Then they have invited friends to

CD

come and look at the menu cards and choose what they would like to eat.

The café is, in effect, relocated to the book area each session that Val and Suzy attend the setting, and no amount of gentle questioning by the practitioners has elicited an answer from the two children about their actions. Their reply to questioning each session is 'We'll put it all back when we've finished', which they always do!

However, as this repeated action means that none of the other children in the setting can use the role-play area as the practitioners had intended, it is decided that Val's and Suzy's actions must be observed and a decision made by staff as to how to approach this apparently inflexible use of equipment.

In one of the books in the staff area there is a chapter about children's repeated patterns of play, and the manager reads this section with her staff at a planning meeting. The staff recognise Val's and Suzy's play as a 'schema' where the children almost compulsively play to learn about how things are transported from one place to another ...

The book suggests ways in which staff can support children who are exploring different concepts through schematic play. One of the other members of staff remembers that there are two other children who regularly build the wooden train track across the entire setting floor and that she cannot recall a train ever being played with on the track! She thinks that perhaps these children are learning about how things join together through a 'connecting' schema. The setting manager then remembers that Suzy's family has just moved house and perhaps that is the reason that the concept of transporting is so important to her. The staff suggest reading *Teddy Bear's Moving Day* to Suzy's group the next day to further help Suzy become comfortable with ideas about moving.

A key feature of this example of creative play is the sensitivity and responsiveness of the staff. On realising that Suzy had important learning needs by playing in the way that she was, staff were eager to support her as best they could. By allowing Suzy to explore her feelings and ideas, they were making a significant contribution to her progress. They then thought of other resources, such as books, that they could use to help her explore and express her ideas about moving house.

(May 2009, pp. 36–7)

A friend tells the story of her two-year-old who would pounce on the newly ironed and folded clothes, ready to be taken upstairs, put them in her doll's pram and transport them across the house.

Cornell drew the most beautiful pictures and unfailingly covered them over in dark paint.

The reasons for this sort of behaviour are, in fact, simple. Schemas are repeated patterns of behaviour, and the term was introduced by Piaget and later developed by Goldschmied and Chris Athey. The first schematic patterns of behaviour are things like sucking and grasping. Babies use these to explore objects, including their own bodies, and they refine and combine these patterns into more and more complex ways of trying to explain their world to themselves. So you see young children walking back and forth across the room, carrying one thing at a time from one place to another. Later the same child might use the doll's pram or an empty box in which to place collections of objects and transport them from place to place. Athey named a number of common schemas, and you may have come across some of the terms in your own work. They include things like going over and under, following a boundary, enveloping and containing space, up and down, rotation, transporting and enveloping. If you are particularly interested in this (and it can be fascinating) read the work of Cathy Nutbrown or Fran Paffard.

What to look out for

- Evidence of repeated patterns or schematic behaviour in babies, toddlers or even older children.

- Evidence of these patterns becoming refined or elaborated.

Implications of this for planning

- Your awareness of repeated patterns of behaviour as relevant and significant ways of learning needs to be shared with your colleagues and with parents and carers. It is important for all of you to take these behaviours seriously and respond appropriately.

- Where you have seen children following schemas you should offer them resources to help them continue their investigations. Children exploring rotation might enjoy having things to spin; those interested in enclosing might enjoy being able to play with animals and fences; those interested in vertical or horizontal schemes might enjoy block play, and so on.

- But most important of all, you need to take this random-seeming behaviour seriously and recognise that it represents a serious attempt by the child to make sense of aspects of the world. So don't tell a child not to paint over a beautiful painting or to stop putting things in the wrong place. Be respectful of these cognitive attempts to make meaning.

10 Questioning and theories

We are very accustomed to questioning children and much less accustomed to encouraging children to question us. In fact, there is evidence that when children are treated respectfully and involved in serious rather than trivial activities they ask questions and come up with theories. Lilian Katz is a powerful supporter of offering children real and **meaningful activities** rather than getting them to collect leaves in order to make a collage or colour in pictures drawn by others. Vygotsky was interested in how children move from holding everyday concepts arrived at through their first-hand experience to being able to think abstractly, and the Reggio Emilia experience shows how children arrive at and then change theories. Rinaldi tells us that when we think of the child as a **competent child** our expectations are raised and the children respond to us differently. She talks of the primitive theories that young children hold and gives an example of the child saying, 'It's raining because the man on TV said it was going to rain.'

Cause and effect and a simple theory! Rinaldi also talks about the respectful educator, one who listens seriously. She gives a wonderful example of three-year-old Federica, who drew a horse and then commented that she had only drawn two legs. So she turned the piece of paper over and drew the other two legs on the back of her drawing. An older child (a five-year-old), also trying to draw a running horse, took the piece of paper with her drawing on, held it against the window and traced on top of her drawing from the other side. In Rinaldi's view this happened because the educator took seriously the child's attempt to make a three-dimensional drawing on a flat piece of paper.

What to look out for

- Evidence that children are asking questions aloud or implicitly. You gather the evidence through listening and watching carefully.

- Evidence that children are making naïve or simple theories about what they think.

Implications of this for planning

- Try and ensure that you encourage children to vocalise as they work and to ask and answer questions as they do so.

- Ensure that a challenge is built into the activities you make available so that children are encountering questions that need answering as they play and work.

- In your planning, based on your observations, pay attention to the expectations you have of the children. Ask yourself if you see them as being competent.

11 Creativity and feelings: emotional intelligence

Daniel Goleman has indicated the importance of what he calls emotional intelligence and believes that it is more closely linked with academic success than factors like IQ level. He defines emotional intelligence as having the necessary emotional strength to withstand the normal stresses and strains of life and believes that children come to have this strength as a result of having established good relationships with others and developing a strong sense of self and confidence. You will know that emotional well-being is a key component of Birth to Three Matters and the EYFS. Sheppy (2009) writes about the importance of emotional development in her book in this series:

PSED

So how are very young children to develop their emotional intelligence? Gooch et al. (2003) say that very early language and involvement in imaginative play provide the opportunities children need to share and try out their feelings. In the first years of their life, children are experiencing everything for the first time, and the way they respond and make sense of what is happening to them and around them is through their emotions. They become aware of their own mood swings and begin to recognise the signs of other people's changing thoughts and feelings. These shifting emotions will first be observed in the home, and if families talk freely about their emotions then children are more likely to be able to share their feelings and to acquire the vocabulary to do so. Males are more likely to learn that it is improper for them to show their emotions, but sometimes the family ethos is such that the members of neither gender express their love or care for each other, either physically or verbally. It is harder for children from such a home to begin to share their feelings, and they can suppress these, often to their detriment, or express them in inappropriate ways. We are all influenced by our early nurturing, and we learn from a very early age how to please the adults we depend on and adapt our behaviour accordingly. We tend to pick up the message from those around us that we need to avoid certain negative emotions and ensure that we can curb or control them when they arise in us. We therefore develop various defence mechanisms to help us cope. As they develop and experience a range of emotions, children become aware of what is expected of them by society in terms of their emotional expression. If they fail to live up to these ideals, they learn what it means to feel guilty. Practitioners need to help children to reflect on their behaviour because only then can they begin to take control of it. Carefully planned stories told with aids such as Persona Dolls (Brown 2001, 2008) and puppets can significantly help this reflection to take place, age appropriately, in a safe environment. The children explore a range of emotions and learn to empathise when someone is anxious or unhappy and can be helped to understand the more difficult concept of how someone can be both worried and cross at the same time. Through participating in such discussion sessions, the children can be encouraged to express their emotions, to empathise with others and to start to solve problems. This is vital for their emotional well-being because the more insight children gain into their own feelings, the more likely it is that they will be able to control their own behaviour. Long (2005: 10–14) talks of the *tags* that practitioners need in order to recognise what might be guiding the children's behaviour. For example, children may have been encouraged to 'be strong'. The strength of this encouragement for them might be that they become self-sufficient and require very little help. They work hard and help others. The downside might be that they find relationships difficult. They would like to be cared for and supported sometimes but find it difficult to ask for help, either practical or emotional, in case they are rejected. Long (2005: 10) says that such a child can then appear 'lonely, cold and aloof towards others'. The challenge for these children is to understand that making mistakes and asking for help is normal. Helping them to see that other children have similar weaknesses can increase their emotional insight and help them to share more of their feelings and not to be afraid that others will reject them. To get the best out of such children, Long advises giving praise and acknowledgement for their consideration, kindness and determination. Pushing them to share their feelings can be counterproductive, but modelling emotional literacy and giving them time on their own can be helpful.

Others *tags* include those who have assimilated the message that they need, above all to 'please others', 'be perfect', 'hurry up' or 'try hard'. Those struggling to live up to such ideals also need to be recognised by the practitioners and given careful attention. Strategies are needed to enable all children not only to discuss their feelings but also to curb their impulses by learning to delay their gratification. Turn-taking games, shared stories and circle-time activities based around the real concerns of the children can all contribute to helping them become emotionally competent. Children need to learn that it is important that we respect and acknowledge each other's feelings and opinions. Some emotions, such as anger, can be very frightening for children who have little experience of the world and do not realise that this is not a permanent state. They need help to understand how such strong emotions can be controlled and managed in future. As the DfES (2007b: 22) says, 'Children who are encouraged to feel free to express their ideas and their feelings, such as joy, sadness, frustration and fear, can develop strategies to cope with new, challenging or stressful situations.'

(Sheppy 2009, pp. 10–12)

Ferre Laevers, in Belgium, also focuses on emotional well-being but he sees it as being related to having a sense of belonging, of vitality, of having fun, and a strong sense of self-confidence and self-esteem. He has developed a system to allow those working with young children to assess and address children's well-being. Nurse (2009) also speaks of well-being, suggesting that self-esteem is essential to well-being and making close links between physical health and mental health. She cites the work of Angela Underdown (2006), one of a growing group of researchers exploring what factors in our society contribute to children's health and well-being, who cite poverty and health inequalities as factors in this. Nurse believes that the child's own sense of self contributes to the sense of well-being but suggests that those working closely to the EYFS guidance should view with care the guidance about child health and development, since this is based on the now discredited age-stage framework, which offers a view of the child with no social, political, economic or cultural context. May (2009) thinks about how the provision of activities allowing children to express their feelings (both positive and negative), as well as their fears, enables them to develop the emotional strength to deal with events, planned and unplanned. She cites an example of children making music from the sounds of the thunder and rain and analyses the effects on the children as follows:

> a frightening experience can become the foundation of a genuinely creative one and help the child to see the storm from a different perspective. In the case of moving house, the experience can be practised over and over again with role play.
>
> (May 2009, p. 20)

For May the explanation lies in the nature of play which gives control to the child.

> This ensures that children have control of the situation until they feel happier about it. It is important that the play does 'integrate' all children's areas of development. For play will only be effective if children can explore what they feel, what they know and what they can do and bring all of these elements to the play. It is because play is able to offer such integration that it is such a powerful tool for exploring feelings, aims, fears and ideas.
>
> (ibid.)

For me, the example of responding to unplanned events in the lives of children is an essential ingredient of responsive teaching. A thunderstorm, a death in the family, a new baby, an accident on the way to the setting, seeing a dog run over – there are dozens of events, small and enormous, in the lives of young children we need to know about, recognise, talk about and equip children to deal with as best we can. In Reggio Emilia too, the well-being of children is regarded as essential and the whole learning process is described as being a creative process. In terms of Rinaldi's thinking this means that children develop the ability to construct new connections between objects and thoughts, and these bring about changes and innovations, taking known elements and creating new ones. For Rinaldi and others creativity is then not just an individual way of thinking but an interactive and social process. You will remember how Malaguzzi talked of 'the hundred languages of children': it is through using these languages that children become able to express their ideas and thoughts and feelings and in doing this create things that are new and challenging in themselves.

What to look out for

- Evidence that children are forming strong relationships with the adults and with one another.

- Evidence that their responses to frustration or perceived failure are appropriate and varied.

- Evidence of children showing self-confidence in their actions and play.

- Evidence that children use different means in order to express their ideas and thoughts and feelings. You will want to see children using words and pictures and sounds and music and movement and everything possible to express themselves.

- Evidence in children's work of things you feel are inventive or innovative.

Implications of this for planning

- Do you plan for children's emotional well-being on a regular basis?

- Do you create a culture of respect for children and for their efforts?

- Do you always plan so that children have access to a range of media in which to express their ideas and feelings and thoughts?

- Do you respond appropriately to the children's work, showing you recognise their uniqueness?

What you have learned

After reading the last two chapters you should have a sense of some of the key ideas that currently inform thinking and discussion about young children, how they learn best and what those involved in their care and education can and should do to ensure that, in the words of the Statutory Framework for the Early Years Foundation Stage, they 'plan and organise their systems to ensure that every child receives an enjoyable and challenging learning and development experience that is tailored to meet their individual needs' (DfES 2007a, p. 37).

Glossary

closed questions: Questions to which one can give a one-word answer – yes or no, for example. They do not allow for dialogue or the exchange of ideas.

competent child: A phrase much used by modern educators, including those in Reggio Emilia, to show the view that human infants are seen as seeking to make sense of the world from birth.

cultural tool: A term coined by Vygotsky. Sometimes referred to as psychological tools, these are the objects and signs and systems developed by human beings over time and within communities to assist thinking. They include things like language, symbols, music, art and others. They are what allow children to move from depending on direct exploration to abstract thought.

eye-pointing: Used by infants before they are able to use speech. This describes how they stare at an object in order to communicate a desire or a need. An important communicative tool.

hundred languages of children: How Malaguzzi described the vast range of ways of expressing ideas and feelings that should be made available to children. So drawing, painting, moving, dancing, speaking, writing, making and so on are all 'languages' in this sense.

integrating mechanism: The phrase used by Tina Bruce to describe her thoughts on play in which she believed that children were able to bring many aspects of their experience to create something new. So play enables children to integrate experiences and ideas.

meaningful activity: This is used to describe activities in which the child can see some purpose rather than an activity where the purpose is unclear. In this way cooking and shopping and writing are meaningful.

mode of learning: People often talk of play as a mode of learning, and what they mean is that it is a way of learning.

monologuing: A clumsy term to describe what children do when they speak aloud the processes they go through. When this stops being spoken aloud it is called 'inner speech', which is synonymous with thinking. Both contrast with social speech, which is speech with others.

play scripts: The way in which a play sequence develops together with the roles, actions and speech that accompany it. No one writes the scripts but the children involved construct these together. A complex task of negotiation and interaction.

pretend play: Sometimes called imaginative or fantasy play, this is where children play out roles from stories or from their imagination.

range of affect: We look to see that children's emotional responses are varied and show a range of moods and responses. We expect to see children sometimes happy, sometimes jealous, sometimes angry, and so on.

role play: Where children play out different roles. Some believe that role play evolves from domestic roles (mum, dad, etc.), through functional roles (doctor, teacher, etc.) to imaginative roles (wizard, dragon, etc.).

sociocultural stance: The values of those who believe that everything has to be analysed according to the society and the culture of the context.

symbolic: Where one thing is used to stand for or symbolise something else.

symbolic play: Play which involves using things to stand for others – a stick for a horse, a cup for a hat, and so on.

The Statutory Framework

Getting it to work for you

As you will almost certainly know, the EYFS became mandatory for schools and all early years providers in OFSTED-registered settings attended by young children in September 2008. The impact of this has been to combine a number of documents and proposals and principles into one framework which provides an overarching structure for the care and education of children from birth to the end of the academic year during which the child has her fifth birthday.

There is much to celebrate in this move and much that causes concern. You will all have copies of the documents that form the Framework within your settings, and if you haven't yet had a chance to read them you should certainly do so in connection with this book. The Framework covers a number of areas described as follows: an introduction to the Framework which looks at context, legal responsibilities and principles; the learning and development requirements; the welfare requirements; and other information, including looking at other legal duties, inspections and regulation, and so on. For our purposes we will confine ourselves to looking in detail at:

- the principles, which are important in defining the scope and ideology underpinning the Framework;
- the large Section 2 which looks at learning and development requirements; and
- a sub-section on organisation.

The aims of the EYFS

The document starts by asserting that it recognises that the early years of a child's life are very important and have a more lasting and powerful influence than successive phases. Much has been written about this, and we know from our own experiences and from being sensitive to the experiences of the children we encounter what truth there is in this. It follows, then, that one of the aims of the EYFS is to ensure that practitioners help children to ultimately meet the five outcomes of *Every Child Matters*. These are, as you know:

- to stay safe;
- to be healthy;
- to enjoy and achieve things;
- to make a positive contribution;
- to achieve economic well-being.

It is tempting to be cynical here and wonder how any of us will ever know if even one of the children we have cared for achieves these long-term goals, and I would be happier with more immediate goals which indicate that we see childhood as a vital phase in its own right and not as preparation for achieving economic well-being. But let's move on.

Within those overarching goals there are some fine points of principle, all of which are important for you to consider in your planning.

1   The first is that some standards need to be set for the learning and devel-opment and care of children outside the home, *making sure that every child makes progress and no child is left behind*. This is something you will need to keep an eye on when you start thinking about planning.

2   The next point is to ensure that all children *experience equality of oppor-tunity and never encounter* **discrimination**. This means that in your plan-ning you must know what experiences each of your key children has had in the sense of knowing about their home language, culture and values.

3   The third point talks about the importance of *building partnerships between professionals (you and your colleagues) and parents*. In terms of your planning, it is important that you think about the ways in which parents can have a voice in your setting. They do, after all, know more about their child than anyone else. And it is important to plan how you

can share your observations and thoughts with them. After all, all parents want the best for their children and often feel sad to miss out on significant moments in learning and development.

4   The fourth point has less importance for you in terms of planning but is highly significant in terms of the whole early years sector. It is the point of *improving quality and* **consistency** throughout the sector. You will note that it does not address one of the issues that most concerns practitioners – that of the discrepancy between the pay and conditions of teachers and of other key workers.

5   The last point is the only one that actually mentions the word 'planning'. It says that practitioners can lay the foundations for future learning by *planning around the individual needs and interests of the child and informed by the use of ongoing observation and assessment.* This, for us, is the crucial point and actually summarises what this book is about. It is not about areas of learning or about early learning goals. It is about you, through paying close attention to what you see and hear children saying and doing, being able to identify what their interests are and to plan from this to take their learning forward.

These issues are clearly addressed in the advice offered by Sheppy (2009) where she says:

> The model set by the staff is very important in this area. It is no use the practitioner expecting the children to include others in their play, to share, to wait for their turn, to be sensitive to the feelings of others, if they consistently ignore a certain child, talk about a member of staff behind their back, or are dismissive of a carer with whom they have close dealings. A team of staff with a strong ethos of care and nurture, and a fierce sense of equality for all, will be in a good position to monitor each other in a supportive and constructive way. Our negative response to a particular child, carer or member of staff might be disguising an underlying prejudice that we are unaware of. We may not even recognise that we are behaving differently towards that person, but if our behaviour has been observed by another member of staff, they have the difficult task of trying to broach the subject with us in a positive way. This is not easy; no one likes to be criticised, and we are all aware that we are far from perfect ourselves, but if the goal is clearly to help everyone to grow

PSED

in respect and care for each other, then such moments can be liberating for all concerned. Once we have recognised a prejudice within ourselves, then we can begin to deal with it. If the children see that it is possible for the adults in the setting to apologise to each other, to work hard at their relationships, to work collaboratively, to listen actively to each other and to change their behaviour when necessary, then they will feel more comfortable about sharing their worries over their own partnerships. They will come to you confidently knowing that all matters of discrimination will be taken seriously and that they can learn to improve their own relationships and develop the skills necessary to work with and not against others.

(Sheppy 2009, pp. 98–9)

 # The EYFS principles

The Statutory Framework document states that effective practice in this stage is built on what they call four *guiding themes*. These themes are said to provide the context for the requirements of the Framework, and the cards relating to these are said to give practitioners 'tips' for what to do to support learning and development and care. You will no doubt have seen the cards which do this. I find this quite disturbing. Supporting the learning and development of young children is not like baking a cake or making a stew and cannot be summed up as a series of recipes. It is intensely difficult work requiring observation and analytical skills, sensitivity to the needs and interests of individual children, skills of working with others, and much more. But let us look at the themes themselves.

1   The first one is called 'A Unique Child', and it is here that the individuality of each child is recognised, and the important fact that each child is a competent learner from birth. This is a recurring theme of this book and one which should underpin your planning. The commitments focused on here look at development, inclusion, safety, health and well-being. This is what Hughes (2009, p. 31) says about this theme:

> This principle highlights a child's natural ability to learn … Even babies of under six months old are actively using their senses to discriminate between what they can recognise and what is unfamiliar. When children are trusted to take safe risks in their play,

PSRN

they learn to think. When children think, they take care and learn skills. When children learn skills, they become resilient, capable, confident and self assured.

2   The second is 'Positive Relationships', which describes how children learn to be strong and independent from a base of what they call loving and secure relationships with parents and/or a key person. No mention is made of the importance of interaction with others apart from these, and one wonders where the influence of friends, siblings, grandparents and others is. The commitments here are respect, **partnership** with parents, supporting learning and the role of the **key person**. Hughes says:

> Every baby and child needs love in order to thrive, and a secure loving relationship is the foundation for all successful learning. We all have to manage the balance between anxiety and curiosity when we are learning something new. It is what drives us all in our learning. However, when anxiety becomes overwhelming, we become frozen with fear and are unable to do anything. When babies and children first come to a setting, whether it is in the home of a childminder, a day-care nursery, a pre-school or a nursery class, they will be feeling frightened and insecure. The most important thing is to help the baby or child settle in with his or her key person. This may take a long time for some children. It does not matter. The time making positive relationships will lead the way to successful learning and happy children ... I refer to the practitioner's role as a 'facilitating' one, which means 'easing the way' in a child's learning. A baby feels secure if you are sitting comfortably nearby when he or she is playing with a treasure basket. Small children will take delight in collecting pebbles or conkers on a walk knowing their key person is with them sharing in their delight. Children learn problem-solving and number skills through their efforts to help their key person in tasks such as setting the table and sharing out food.
>
> (Hughes 2009, p. 32)

3   The third is 'Enabling Environment', which, you will not be surprised to learn, focuses on the key role the environment is said to play in supporting and extending learning. The **enabling environment** is a very Piagetian

approach, ignoring the vital role that the social and the cultural play. The commitments here are observation, assessment and planning; support for every child; the learning environment; and the wider environment including **transitions**, **continuity** and **multi-agency working**.

4   The last is 'Learning and Development', which recognises that all children learn in different ways and at different rates and that all areas of learning are interconnected and equally important.

We haven't yet talked about **holistic** learning, so perhaps this is the place to do so. Most of the people who have looked at early learning have observed that young children do not learn in subjects or in learning areas.

Let's look at some examples to illustrate this. As you read each one ask yourself these questions: 'Is this child learning? What learning area does her learning fall into?'

● Four-year-old Lucca goes out into the garden and takes notice of the plants and thinks about them. Perhaps he is asking himself, 'Why is this flower pink and that one over there orange?' or 'How did this plant come to be here?' or 'Why is this plant moving more in the wind than that one?'

● Poppy, at 18 months, has become a problem solver and an imitator; when the carer is cleaning she follows her around with her own cloth and is desperate to have a go with the broom and the dustpan. Her carer reported that when she wanted something out of reach she dragged a chair across the floor and then attempted to climb up on it (Smidt 2006, p. 44).

● Malika seems to be exploring the way in which some things will dissolve and others won't. She spends time putting water into some sand and stirring it. Then she tries putting water into gravel and stirring it to see what happens (Smidt 2006, p. 44).

● When Ola was ten weeks old she spent hours watching the mobile over her cot. She watched the movements with intense concentration. Some months later she started to enjoy some simple games that she played with her big sister, who would hide her toys and say 'all gone' and then make them pop up again. Ola always shrieked with delight (Smidt 2006, p. 44).

I have no doubt that each of these children is deeply involved in looking at things and trying things out and making up theories and asking questions. They are certainly learning. But can we say that Lucca is involved in biology or botany, that Poppy is an apprentice cleaner or that Malika is a little scientist?

And what on earth could we say about Ola and the area of her learning? It is very difficult for those of us involved with very young children to think about their learning in learning areas, and this is a structural constraint within the Framework that you will have to find a way of working around. When you start to examine the *Practice Guidance for the Early Years Foundation Stage* (DfES 2008) you will see that a lot of twiddling has been necessary to make the learning of babies, in particular, fit into the learning areas. But what is useful is the column telling you, the practitioner, what to look and listen for and take note of. This is something I suggest you refer to often since it will help you know what to look out for and this will enhance your abilities to plan.

The first section ends with a statement which both delights and concerns me and I shall quote it in full:

> The EYFS sets standards to enable early years providers to reflect the rich and personalised experience that many parents give their children at home. Like parents, providers should deliver individualised learning, development and care that enhances the development of the children in their care and gives those children the best possible start in life. Every child should be supported individually to make progress at their own pace and children who need extra support to fulfil their potential should receive special consideration. All providers have an equally important role to play in children's early years experiences – for example, a childminder who sees a child for two hours a day should consider what a child's individual needs are at that time of day, and ensure that the provision they deliver is both appropriate to those needs and complementary to the education and care provided in the child's other setting(s). All types of providers have the potential to deliver the EYFS to an excellent standard.
>
> (DfES 2007a, p. 9)

It sounds wonderful, doesn't it? Whoever you are and wherever you work you will provide an individual curriculum to each child, carefully matched to the needs of the child at any particular time. The reality, I fear, will be very different, and it is difficult to imagine how some practitioners – particularly those working on their own – will be able to do this. But for most of us this paragraph gives us permission to do exactly what we are recommending in this book: pay attention to what children already know, have already learned, can already do and are now interested in, and provide opportunities related to these things in order to take the child's learning and development forward.

Planning and assessment systems

Under a section in the Framework called 'Organisation' we come across this recommendation: 'Providers must plan and organise their systems to ensure that every child receives an enjoyable and challenging learning and development experience that is tailored to meet their individual needs' (p. 37).

The Framework then goes out to outline what such a system should look like:

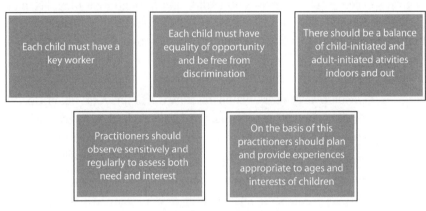

The Framework's outline

There is also a section on things providers need to consider as they set up an observation and planning and assessment process:

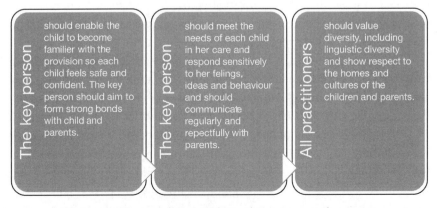

Things providers need to consider as they set up an observation and planning and assessment process

I have edited this slightly and you can find the original on page 37 of the Framework. I have left out the requirement to ensure that children who come to your setting with little or no English can learn English through a range of meaningful contexts. I have left this out of the chart not because I feel it is not important, but rather the opposite. This, for me, is a crucial and vital point. The way in which I interpret this is that **plurilingual** young children (which means those children who have more than one language) should never be put in **withdrawal groups** or given formal English language teaching. They will learn English through their interactions with English speakers, both children and adults, and through their play, listening to stories, having resources like story props to help them understand, and through meaningful activities. Bradford reminds us of the importance of story sacks:

- Develop a good selection of story sacks in your setting to support storytelling activities. (NB: it is much cheaper to make your own than to buy commercially.) Remember to include traditional tales and multicultural tales as part of the collection.

- Allow story sacks to go home with the children. Invite parents and carers to take part in a story sack workshop so that they know how to use them supportively with their children.

(Bradford 2009, p. 91)

It is important to remember that allowing speakers of other languages to use their languages in the setting will both show respect for the children and their languages and cultures and also enable children to continue to learn in their first and strongest language.

Much has been written about the effect of ignoring what children bring with them from home and their communities to schools and settings. Most obvious is when young children who do not speak English are treated as not being capable or competent learners. Jean Conteh, at a talk in London in May 2008, told the story of how one of her students had written an essay on her early years at school and how she was made to feel stupid, being, at first, the only Gujarati speaker in her class. This child could think; she could speak more than one language. Yet the effect of having her prior knowledge ignored was to make her have no sense of her own abilities. She began to wish away her culture, her language, her very self.

The learning and development requirements

You will know that there are learning and development requirements that you must deliver, regardless of the type or size of funding of your setting. This is laid down in law and, as we have already said, you will have received *Practice Guidance for the Early Years Foundation Stage* (DfES 2008), together with supporting resources, and you can always refer to these. Here, just to set the scene, are some points to keep in mind.

A reminder that all children must be regarded as *competent learners* from birth. All learn in different ways. You must observe carefully and sensitively in order to build a continually evolving picture of each of your key children's interests, needs and progress. Bromley (2006) reminds us that 'all children, however young, must be given the chance to be seen as writers from the very beginning' (p. 15).

1 You are told to plan for activities and experiences across *all areas of learning*. But do remember that learning in the early years is essentially holistic, involving many different spheres of knowledge or learning areas.

2 You are reminded that the Childcare Act 2006 provided for all learning and development to address three elements:

(a) the *early learning goals*, which are the knowledge, skills and understanding which those writing the Act have decided all children should have acquired by the end of the academic year in which they have their fifth birthdays;

(b) the *educational programmes*, which they define as the topics or matters and the skills and processes which should be taught to young children;

(c) the *assessment arrangements*, which are the arrangements each class or school or setting puts in place to assess whether children have reached the early learning goals or to identify their achievement to date.

3 You are reminded that you have to *cover the six learning areas* and that these should not be seen as discrete or isolated from one another. Each is equally important and they are interdependent.

4 Finally, you are reminded that all these areas must be delivered through *planned, purposeful play, with a balance of adult-led and child-initiated activities*. We have talked about this issue earlier in this book, and you will

need to think carefully about how play, which is by definition self-chosen, can be defined as planned play and why the word 'purposeful' is needed if we consider play to be what children do when they are able to follow up their own interests and concerns. This makes it purposeful. You need to think, also, about whether the balance of child-led and adult-led activities should be the same for babies as for toddlers, for toddlers as for older children. We will discuss this in more detail in the chapters that follow.

What you have learned

This chapter has been a summary of some of the principles and key points of the new Framework. Much will have been familiar to you, but hopefully what this chapter has given you is an understanding of what you are required to do in terms of planning – which is the subject of this book.

Glossary

consistency: You probably know the meaning of this word: it means ensuring that things remain the same. The importance for us is in terms of how carefully we work to ensure that the experience of the child is smooth, so that new members of staff can slot into established routines and transitions are carefully and sensitively managed.

continuity: The meaning of this is probably apparent but it is important to remember that being able to follow through interests and learn in any depth requires continuity in terms of having time and in terms of minimising the number of changes young children experience.

discrimination: You may think that very young children don't discriminate against others or notice when they are discriminated against, but this is not the case. One of the essential principles is that all children (and that includes their languages and culture) should be treated with respect and all children should be helped to learn to respect others. *Perhaps one of the most important aspects of your roles.*

enabling environments: This is based on Piaget's view that a stimulating learning environment alone could facilitate learning. Many people feel there are things missing from this view – particularly the vital role of others in learning. Others feel that it has a very Western view implying that 'rich' environments are better for learning than 'poor' environments, and there is no evidence to support this.

holistic: The EYFS places great emphasis on the six learning areas but does point out that these are not separate and discrete but overlap. Many thinkers believe that learning, particularly in the early years, is holistic – which means that young children do not learn in separate subject areas. *An important point to remember.*

key worker/person: I am sure you don't need this word in a glossary but I include it just to remind you that this key person (the term used) is the one who should help the baby or child become familiar with the setting and to feel confident in it. She should establish a strong bond with her children and is the one who is required to meet the needs of each child in her care. But the key person, in group care, is not the only person to interact with the child or to observe or plan for the child. In group care, key workers work in teams and team planning and discussion is essential to successful working.

multi-agency working: This refers to different experts, practitioners or specialists working together for the well-being of the child.

partnerships: Again, a term you don't need explaining, but included here as a reminder of the importance of all early years practitioners working in close and equal partnerships with parents/ carers.

plurilingual: The current term used to talk about those who speak and/or read and/or write more than one language. In this country and in your provision you will encounter children who are plurilingual.

transition: This refers to when children move from one group to another or one setting to another. There is the huge transition from home to setting and various other transitions during the life of the child. All are potentially difficult, sometimes traumatic, and all need to be planned for and handled with sensitivity.

withdrawal groups: Where children – often those who have English as an additional language – are removed from the mainstream group and given small group support. This is damaging. It makes these children feel even more different and often inferior, and it removes all the peer models for using English.

5 | Building a planning system

Before you read this chapter please look again at the diagram of the planning cycle below to remind yourself of the process. It is essential to keep reminding yourself that planning is part of an ongoing cycle and that today's plan in action leads directly to the plan for tomorrow: tomorrow's plan in action leads directly to the plan for the day after. You start by observing the children, taking notes on what you see and hear. You analyse this, looking for key points about children's interests, advances, achievements or struggle.

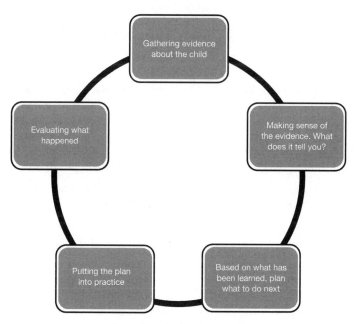

The ongoing planning cycle

On the basis of that you plan what to offer next. You then set up the activity you have planned, together with the resources, physical and human. Then you observe what happens in the activity and the whole process starts again.

I know that many practitioners, particularly those who work alone, like childminders, find the whole idea of the statutory nature of the EYFS very threatening. At first sight, it is. The thought of having to monitor each child in terms of reaching 69 learning goals is terrifying. And the implications of having to write things down are also frightening in terms of how to manage the process. How do you manage to observe and record what you see and hear as well as play with the children, prepare their food, get them off to sleep, sing to them, read to them, help them when they struggle, comfort them when they are distressed and interact with them in different ways throughout the day? The aim of this chapter is to show you how some of what you are being asked to do really does build on existing good practice and is possible as long as you take the trouble to put in place a workable system.

Vicky Hutchin (2007) has come up with a set of principles to underpin practice. These are so important and useful that I take the liberty of repeating them here. They are presented here quite baldly, and if you want to know more about her views do read her very readable and useful book.

1   *The starting point for planning and assessment is the child and not a set of **predetermined goals**.* This means that you must start by looking at and listening to children and not by looking at the EYFS Development Matters, Early Learning Goals or EYFS Profile scale points. These can be used to inform what you observe but not to dictate what to look out for.

2   Observations and assessments must always *look at what children can do* – at their achievements – and not at what they cannot do. You need to hold high expectations for what children could do. You need to avoid labelling or stereotyping children. You need to respect and value diversity.

3   You should *observe children as part of what you do on a daily basis.* It should just be part of what you routinely do.

4   Ensure that you *observe children through the **routines** of the day*, at play, listening to stories, in the garden or at playtime. So ensure that you *observe them in self-chosen activities and in adult-led activities.*

5   When you observe children, ensure that you *pay attention to and take note of their interests and passions and concerns as well as what strategies they use as learners*.

6   Just observing and writing down what you see and hear is not enough. You must *think about what you have seen and heard in terms of what you know about how children learn and develop, and use the information to inform your planning.*

7   You should do your best to *invite parents to be part of the assessment process*. They are experts in terms of knowing about their own children and their contribution is essential.

8   *When children are able to make choices and give reasons for these, do invite them to be involved in talking about how well they are doing.* Invite them to pick something they are very pleased with or tell you about what they think they did well.

9   *All those involved with each child should be able to contribute to the records you keep* of children's learning and development, and parents and children themselves should have easy access to them. With babies and toddlers you might want to learn from the example of Reggio Emilia, where there is a photograph of each child displayed on the wall together with a daily space for key workers to record what the child did, significant moments or just delightful details. These are designed to make parents feel more a part of the child's life at the setting. Or you might want to refer to the wonderful Learning Stories cited by Stella Louis later in this book or the individual Profile books which individual children, together with the key person, share with their parents and other children at Andover Children's Centre, which is also to be found later in this book.

KUW

10   *Keep dated and* **annotated** *examples of children's work* together with observation notes and comments. Update these regularly and review and summarise them.

11   Ensure that you *track all your key children*.

These principles are important and they should make you appreciate that planning and assessment are part of good practice as long as the planning and assessment start with the child and not with the targets or learning goals.

So keep doing what you are good at – and build on that.

How to make observation and recording possible

At first sight the EYFS seems to be trying to change the roles of nannies, childminders and crèche workers into something formal and distant. You all have particular reasons for having chosen to work with young children and all have some experience to build on. Since the new Framework is statutory, it is important to adapt and work it to meet *your* needs and build on *your* strengths. Remember what you are good at and don't lose sight of it. We can all learn new skills and all benefit from the experiences of others. You are all good at taking notice of what children do and say. This is the very essence of what you do in your work. You know the children in your care and are, by definition, interested in what they do and say. Put another way, you pay attention to them. So what you have to do now is find or create a system to help you make notes of what you hear and say within the natural routines and rituals of the day. Here are some points to help you do this.

Observation notes can be very detailed, and you might decide to do an in-depth observation if you are interested in something special, but day-by-day observation notes should **summarise** what you have seen and heard. You are making note of something **significant** – some achievement of the observed child. Here are some examples to read. As you do so, see if you can identify why each might be described as being significant.

Kelly held her bottle by herself, using both hands.

Darinder and Iqbal took turns on the scooter.

Marko wrote the first letter of his name.

Sukie smiled at me for the first time.

Poppy pretended to read.

Julio used one of the wooden blocks as a telephone.

Each of those statements is perfectly clear. Each describes *something significant*. Each can (by the way) also be seen as a step on the way to achieving those dreaded learning goals. What is missing is any indication of when each took place, and this is relevant if you are using your observations both to plan from and to show progress. So here they are again, this time dated.

13 February 2008   Kelly held her bottle by herself, using both hands.

12 February 2008   Darinder and Iqbal took turns on the scooter.

16 January 2008   Marko wrote the first letter of his name.

21 February 2008   Sukie smiled at me for the first time.

22 February 2008   Poppy pretended to read a book.

03 March 2008   Julio used one of the wooden blocks as a telephone.

Each of these small observations was written by key workers using Post-it notes and then placed in the folder for the child. But before they were put in the folder the key worker read through them, thought about what they told her about the child's learning and interests and used them for planning, like this. The planning bits are in italic.

13 February 2008   Kelly held her bottle by herself, using both hands.

She is being independent and I want to encourage this, so I must ensure that I give her the bottle to hold again tomorrow and perhaps offer her a spoon to see what she makes of that.

12 February 2008   Darinder and Iqbal took turns on the scooter.

This is the first time they have shared. So I will plan to put out some other toys they will have to share during this week.

16 January 2008   Marko wrote the first letter of his name.

I told his mum and she gave him a huge hug. Tomorrow I am going to get him to see if he can find that initial letter of his name in the big register I have written up. We have three other children whose names start with M.

21 February 2008   Sukie smiled at me for the first time.

I will smile back! I will also try and see who or what else she smiles at.

22 February 2008   Poppy pretended to read a book.

First time I have seen her do this. Will watch more carefully to see if she holds the book the right way up and turns the pages. I might sit with her and ask her if I can share the book with her. I want her to know that I have noticed that she likes to act like a reader.

3 March 2008   Julio used one of the wooden blocks as a telephone.

From my reading I know that this is a significant moment. He is using one thing to stand for another – as a symbol. I will look to see what other things he uses as symbols and perhaps start using some symbols myself.

So we have seen how daily and brief observations can build up a picture of the child as learner and contribute to planning. We will now move on to linking this with the demands and requirements of the Early Years Foundation Stage.

 # Linking this back to the EYFS

In your work as a teacher, childminder, nursery worker or any other sort of practitioner, you will almost always start with the child and begin by watching her and listening to her in order to get a sense of that child as an individual and unique learner. Writing down what you see and hear is not difficult. Thinking about it or analysing it can be more difficult. The Practice Guidance for the EYFS offers you some ways of thinking about how to analyse what you see and hear and linking this to the learning areas and other aspects of the EYFS. I invited a friend, Eva, who works with very young children, to use the Practice Guidance in order to help her analyse the examples we have just looked at. Here are her comments.

Kelly

You will remember Kelly, who held her bottle by herself for the first time when she was ten months old. Her key worker thought that this marked a step in becoming independent and wanted to encourage this.

I turned to the self-care section of 'Personal, Social and Emotional Development' in the Practice Guidance and noted that Kelly was at least at the level of other children of the same age in terms of her development of independence. I was also interested in commenting on her use of two hands, and in this case I looked at the 'Using Equipment and Materials' section of 'Physical Development'. In both cases I felt that Kelly's behaviour was pleasingly in advance of the ages cited in the document.

Sukie

Sukie smiling at the key worker for the first time.

I thought Sukie was showing a social response and was surprised not to be able to find this in the Practice Guidance. Nonetheless, I felt this was significant and kept the observation note. I trusted my own judgement and my own experience. I advise other workers to do the same. Value your own experience and judgement.

Poppy

Poppy's key worker was convinced that the example showed her knowledge of how books work.

I also think this shows Poppy's developing understanding of how books work and found this in the section on reading in the 'Communications, Language and Literacy' area. I wanted to know what exactly the child was doing and made a note to suggest to the key worker that she check that Poppy was turning the pages and holding the book the correct way up. It came as no surprise to find out that she had already done this.

The planning process so far

In terms of the planning process we have:

1   considered how we can summarise what is seen and heard and what seems to be significant;

2   reminded ourselves to date each observation so that we can build a developing picture of the learner;

3   read through the notes to think about what they show and why that matters using personal judgement on referring to the EYFS Practice Guidance;

4   on the basis of our reflection, decided to either keep the observation note or discard it;

5   thought about what to plan next for the child concerned.

The following figure summarises the planning process up to this point:

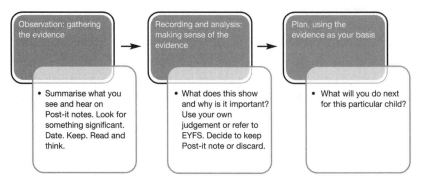

Summary of the planning process

The resource and time implications

For a system to be **manageable** it must be *simple*, **transparent** *and well-resourced*. It must be simple enough to allow you to do it without strain, transparent so that someone who stands in for you can operate it, and well-resourced so you don't run out of Post-it notes or whatever else you use.

1   Whatever you decide to use to jot down observations must be available to you at all times. Try and jot down your notes as you interact with or observe the children. *Have Post-it notes or their equivalent in all areas* or in your pocket. You may need to develop your own shorthand.

2   *Date* each one.

3   Make time as soon as possible after you have made the notes to *read through them* or, if you work with others, to *discuss them*. In some nurseries and settings there is a ten-minute focused session at the end of each day to plan the next day. This has to be carefully managed so that you stick to the agenda.

Here is an example of what they do at the Godolphin Children's Centre:

> We use specially printed observation forms. Each one is A5 in size and you are reminded to just jot down significant moments and there is a place for the date and for you to initial it so everyone knows whose notes they are. This is because whoever is in that area or at

the activity can jot down anything they notice that is significant. This figure is an example of a blank form.

Date   Initial
Activity

Children involved

What you saw and heard

A blank observation form

And here is the procedure for completing these summarised:

1   Put the date and your initials on the form before the day actually begins.
2   Fill in the type of activity and names of children who have joined it as the activity starts. We don't all manage that!

The next figure shows two completed forms.

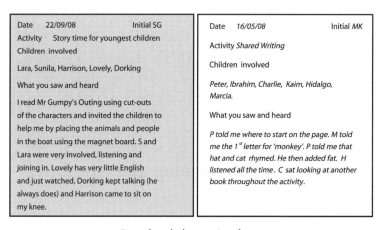

Date   22/09/08   Initial SG
Activity   Story time for youngest children
Children involved

Lara, Sunila, Harrison, Lovely, Dorking

What you saw and heard

I read Mr Gumpy's Outing using cut-outs of the characters and invited the children to help me by placing the animals and people in the boat using the magnet board. S and Lara were very involved, listening and joining in. Lovely has very little English and just watched. Dorking kept talking (he always does) and Harrison came to sit on my knee.

Date   16/05/08   Initial MK

Activity Shared Writing

Children involved

Peter, Ibrahim, Charlie, Kaim, Hidalgo, Marcia.

What you saw and heard

P told me where to start on the page. M told me the 1st letter for 'monkey'. P told me that hat and cat rhymed. He then added fat. H listened all the time. C sat looking at another book throughout the activity.

Completed observation forms

You might be interested to know that we spent most of the ten-minute meeting discussing the story group for the next day because SG, who made the grey observation notes, felt that Dorking and Harrison, in particular, need to be with a different and smaller group.

We all meet for a ten-minute meeting at the end of the morning and share what we have noticed. We then talk briefly and sometimes we ask and answer these questions to help focus our discussion:

- What activity are we leaving out again tomorrow? Why?

- What are we adding to an activity or taking away from it tomorrow? Why?

- What new activity, if any, are we offering tomorrow? Why?

- Who will be our target children to observe tomorrow?

We also plan which adults will be where and doing what. I might be a play partner or I might be leading an activity, and so might my colleagues. Or we might be observing, or setting up, or interacting with specific children, or organising an outing or a visit, or model-ling something specific. After the meeting we give the key worker for each child who has been mentioned a copy of the observation note to file in the child's folder.

Now this is our day-to-day planning and it is where we might or might not make changes to what we planned for the week. On the day on which MK noted a child's interest in rhymes, we decided that one of us would tell a rhyming story to a group and invite the child concerned to join us.

You will see that this group of staff have discussed and planned how their observations can affect what they do every day based on what they have seen, heard, discussed and understood. It is a good, if not a unique, example.

The next step in the planning and assessment process

Let us summarise where we are up to:

1   You have observed a child or a group of children, paying attention to what they are interested in and noticing what they say and do.

2   You have made notes summarising this and have dated your notes.

3   Either alone or with your co-workers, you have briefly discussed or reviewed what you have seen and decided what to set up the next day to meet the needs or interests you have noted. What happens next?

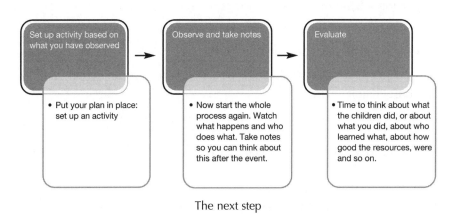

The next step

There is very little new here. On the basis of what you noticed and discussed you set either a new activity or the same activity. And now you start the whole process again. You watch what happens as the children take part in or reject the activity you set up and you make notes. The point of showing this as another cycle is purely to indicate that this simple process of observe–analyse–plan–observe allows you to monitor the progress of children and also to evaluate the effectiveness of your planning, resourcing and interacting in taking learning and development further.

Exploring the notion of evidence

We have talked about collecting **evidence** through observation and I want to look at this in more detail. I want you to be sure about what might constitute evidence and how it can be used to show development, progress, learning or a significant moment.

The evidence you are looking for is evidence of learning or development. This could refer to learning intellectual things, like how to read or write or count. It could refer to learning social things, like how to interact and share and belong and make relationships. It could be emotional things, like how to express love or fear or anger. It could refer to learning something for the first time or to improving skills already learned. In short, you might be looking for any or all of the following:

1   evidence of a child working at or solving a problem: holding a theory or **making a hypothesis**, being curious or asking questions;
2   evidence of a child expressing feelings or ideas;
3   evidence of a child communicating effectively and developing relationships;
4   evidence of a child developing a new skill or refining an existing skill, or consolidating learning;
5   evidence of a child making a significant leap in learning.

Now let us look at each one in more detail and illustrate these with examples.

Evidence of a child working at or solving a problem

What might show that the child is working at or solving a problem, or holding a theory, or making a hypothesis, or being curious and questioning?

● You would look out for the child being deeply involved and spending considerable time working at something.
● The child might say something which helps you to know what she is paying attention to or concerned with.
● The child might produce something which illustrates the process gone through – a model or a drawing or a piece of work or a construction, and so on.
● A child who has made up a hypothesis or a guess about how something works would most probably be involved in carrying out a series of tasks designed to test this hypothesis. Again, your role is to be attentive and tuned in to what it is the child is doing. Based on this, you may be able to work out what the hypothesis is.

The following examples all illustrate aspects of this. The first comes from Hughes (2009).

PSRN

Tom reaches a cup

Even before babies can walk or talk they are setting themselves problems to solve. For problem-solving is about having a goal in mind and working out how to achieve that goal. Indeed, children in their play and normal everyday life are constantly setting themselves challenges which are, in effect, difficult goals. No wonder life is so exciting! I once observed a toddler named Tom, who wanted a cup from a high shelf in the kitchen. His mother was not readily available so Tom dragged a chair towards the worktop and proceeded to clamber on to the chair. He then climbed on to the surface of the worktop, from where he could now successfully pick up his self-chosen cup. He then put the cup on to the worktop and reversed the climbing process till he was back on the floor. He could now reach the cup and looked deeply satisfied as he took it to his mother. Needless to say, the chair was not returned! We might not approve of his strategy (with our adult eyes worrying about physical danger) but we cannot deny his satisfaction at achieving his goal by himself.

This short story illustrates a key element in problem-solving, and that is planning. The planning stages are as follows:

- Having a goal. Tom wants the cup.

- Seeing an obstacle. It's out of his reach on a high shelf.

- Working out a strategy. Tom drags a chair and climbs up to the worktop.

- Achieving the goal. Tom can now reach and have his chosen cup.

In this example, there was no other way, in Tom's mind, to get the cup (without the aid of his mother) other than to work out the 'chair strategy'.

(Hughes 2009, pp. 14–15)

The other examples are all based on the personal observations of colleagues and friends.

Melinda's theory

The children had been washing the dolls in one of the low sinks in the nursery. Melinda put her ear to the plughole and seemed to be listening to the water as it ran out.

The very experienced nursery teacher watched this, fascinated, and took a photograph of it. Later she said to Melinda, 'I saw you listening to the water going down the plughole.'

'Yes,' replied the child. 'I wanted to hear if I could tell where it went. I thought I would hear it going into the sea.'

Bola and his seeds

Bola and his friend had planted a seed out in the garden and he went out every day to see what had happened to it. One day he saw a tiny green shoot and the next day he went outside with a ruler. When he came back into the room he drew something on a piece of paper and wrote a symbol beside it. The practitioner made a note of this, plus a comment which read, 'He is using the ruler to measure his plant and I think he invented something to be a number. I will watch and see if he does this again.'

Ryan and Mehmet play with blocks

Ryan and Mehmet are in the block play area. They are building together and assisting one another. The practitioner overhears Ryan say to Mehmet, 'If you hold this one I can put another one on top to balance.'

This is evidence of several things. Both children are sharing the problem to be solved. They are collaborating. Ryan actually asks for help by vocalising his thoughts.

Marko's monologue

Marko is making something in the making area and talks himself through the process. 'I need another one of these ... use some glue ... that doesn't work ... try stronger glue ... '

This is evidence of Marko using spoken language to help explain to himself what he is doing in solving the problem he has set himself.

Zeynep writes a letter

Zeynep is writing a letter to a friend, using made-up writing. When she wants to put it in an envelope for her friend she goes over to the tray where the children keep their things and carefully copies the letters that make up her friend's name.

This is evidence that Zeynep knows that writing serves several purposes and she is making up letters and letter-like shapes in the process of working out how writing works. When she faces the problem of how her friend will know it is for her, she arrives at the decision to copy her friend's name in real letters.

Donna using her hands

Donna has a stick in each hand and wants to hold another one. She puts one down, picks up a new one and puts it in her mouth, and then picks up the original. She has one in each hand and one in her mouth. This seems such a simple thing, but it illustrates real problem solving in a child who is just 13 months old. A practitioner wanting to record this could just note it or take a photograph of it.

So we have seen that evidence can be collected as observation notes, photographs or actual pieces of work. All must be dated.

Evidence of a child expressing feelings or ideas

What might show if the child is expressing feelings or ideas?

- You would look to see how engaged in the task the child is. It is likely that a child who is trying to express powerful feelings or ideas will be deeply involved.

- In genuine dialogue with the child, either during the task or when it has been completed, you might gain some insights into what her intentions were. But take care not to ask meaningless questions like 'What is this?' If you focus on what you see and what you think the child is doing, you might get a very insightful response.

Here are some examples, again based on the notes of friends and colleagues.

Tad's angry lines

Tad took a thick black pen and drew very bold and angry strokes on a piece of paper. He then screwed up the piece of paper, took another piece of paper and chose a red pen and drew some more bold strokes on this sheet. Then he stood back, smoothed out the crumpled piece of paper, went to fetch the glue and stuck the two pictures together. The practitioner who is his key worker said that she felt that this showed his anger. She knew that his mother had been taken into hospital in the previous week and was not home yet.

Maria's doll play

Maria was experiencing extreme pressures at home and her key worker was carefully watching her at play with the characters in the doll's house. The practitioner noted in her observation notes that this three-year-old was using the doll's house figures to re-enact some of the dreadful things going on at home.

Not Now, Bernard

The class teacher read the children the story of *Not Now, Bernard* (McKee 1996) and asked the children afterwards if any of them had ever felt jealous. In the discussion that took place, children spontaneously made links with other emotions – fear, anger, loneliness, and so on.

Singing and smiling

Jenna and Sonya (aged two and a half) held hands and went out into the garden, singing and smiling. The practitioner took a photograph of the children and dated it and put one copy in each child's folder. She felt it showed their expression of feeling happy, secure and safe in a peer relationship.

Evidence of a child communicating effectively and developing relationships

What would show that the child is communicating effectively with another child or adult or making a relationship with another child or an adult?

This is something you would see in action. You might see an infant initiating an exchange by making sounds and waiting for a response. Or you might see an infant smiling at someone familiar. You might see a baby communicating a need or desire by eye-pointing or pointing. You might hear a child asking for help, or a child giving help to another child. You might see children sharing and negotiating and speaking and listening. You might record this in an observation note.

Evidence of a child developing a new skill or refining an existing skill, or consolidating learning

What would show that a child has developed a new skill or is refining an existing skill or consolidating previous learning?

● Here you would be looking out for what we call **milestones** or sig-nificant moments – the first time the child displays that she can do something.

● Or we might see a child who has recently acquired a new skill practising that skill over and over again in order to refine or perfect it.

Here are some small vignettes for you to read. As you do so, think about whether this could be labelled as a milestone or as the refinement of an existing skill.

● Min Duc used a paintbrush today for the first time.

● Shumi went on the trike today for the first time and was so pleased with herself that she sang all the time she was on it.

● Hardeep can't move away from the making table. Since she learned how to use scissors she spends all day, every day, cutting out.

- Rita has learned to write her name and she writes it on anything she finds – paper, cardboard, the painting paper and her book. Her mum found her starting to write it on her bedroom wall!

- Danielle has fallen in love with the modelling table and plays with clay or Plasticine all the time. Every day I see her using a new tool. To date she has used the rolling pin, the pastry cutter, the skewer to make holes, the cheese grater to grate the dough, the paintbrush to make it wet, a plastic knife to cut it up. At first I thought this was random behaviour but I have decided she is refining her skills at using a range of tools.

- Manna spent more than an hour in the home corner and I saw her use the dustpan and brush to clean the table, the broom to sweep the floor, the cloth to wipe the surfaces. I saw her pretend to spray something out of a wooden block as she carried on cleaning.

What have you learned?

In this chapter you have learned something about how to set up a **system** so that the observation you are required to do is manageable. Do remember that although you do have to keep a **record** of children's progress, the way you do it and when you do it is up to you. If you are a **single worker** caring for children you have to manage your time to fit this in. Do try and acquire a digital camera because this makes some aspects of recording easier, and talk to others doing the same work as you in order to find out how they manage. But most of all, remember to start with the child and not with any target or goal.

Glossary

annotated: This refers to what you should do when you notice something significant in a child's work and you write down what is significant. This is annotating an example.

evidence: The notes and comments and bits of work or photographs you gather to show progress. These are the things you analyse and annotate and against which you plan

making a hypothesis: When someone comes up with a theory or an explanation for something they think and can then test out.

manageable: This term is used here with regard to a planning system and indicates that the system you develop and use should be something that allows you to work effectively, doing what is required but without compromising your principles or ideals.

milestones: Usually refers to the first time the child does something significant – things like the child's first step, first word, sitting up unaided, and so on.

predetermined goals: Goals or targets that are decided beforehand.

record: What you do when you write down something.

routines: These usually refer to the regular occurrences that mark out life. For babies there are many of these, and they include things like eating, sleeping and having nappy changes. As the child gets older the routines take up less time, meaning there is more time for activities.

significant: Something that is significant shows something special.

single worker: This is used to describe those of you working alone and without colleagues on a daily basis.

summarise: When you bring together evidence and arrive at some conclusion or when you express what you think in one or two phrases.

system: A set of routines which you create in order to simplify what you are required to do. In this chapter we have been talking about a planning system.

transparent: In this context it means obvious and apparent to others. So your observation system should be usable by someone who has to fill in for you and understandable by anyone who reads your notes.

6 Significant moments

In this chapter we are going to look at how you can identify significant moments in learning, record them and use them to build records of children's progress. In doing this we are going to examine a number of case studies showing how those working in a range of settings are doing this.

In many settings, attempts are made to build records of individual children's progress and to make them into booklets or store them in files and ensure that even the youngest children have access to them. In the best practice you can hear the voices of both the children and their parents in these books. What is possible in group settings is, of course, different from what is possible for childminders, and what is possible in schools is different from what is possible in children's centres. But the EYFS does try and ensure that all children have their learning and development tracked and recorded wherever they are cared for.

In this chapter you can read about how different practitioners manage recording children's progress as they search for significant moments. You will find the words of Genie who is a childminder, Roberto who is a teacher working in a children's centre, Sue who is head of a children's centre, Angelina who is the Foundation Stage Co-ordinator in a primary school **Foundation Stage Unit**, and Denise who is an advisory teacher who brings with her specialist experience through her own training in New Zealand.

Genie records the progress of her children

Let us start by looking at what one childminder, Genie, does in terms of recording children's progress. Here is what she says:

I have been a childminder for years ... started when my kids were young and have just carried on. I think I do it because I just enjoy being with children and find them fascinating. People have suggested I become a teacher but I don't want to. I like being independent and I like working alone. I would hate the routines of the school and would miss being with babies and toddlers. So it suits me. And although I resisted the EYFS at first – and still think much in it is ridiculous – tracking the progress of the children makes absolute sense to me because I have always done it. I have to keep the parents informed about how the children are getting on. After all, they are the parents and I am in the privileged position of seeing significant moments in *their* children's learning and development. So I have always made sure to talk to parents when they bring or collect the children. What is new to me is recording my thoughts – writing things down. I recently bought a digital camera and now I use it throughout the day to record anything that interests me or seems significant. Here are some of the things I have photographed in the last month or so.

- I took a photo of Evelina's first step. I wanted her mum to see this! I thought she might feel sad about missing it!

- I photographed Jojo building a tower. He worked alone and spent nearly 40 minutes doing it. I wanted his parents to see the end product but also to know how hard he worked and with what concentration.

- I had to take a photo of Renata after she had fallen asleep on the floor, holding on to a story book I had had to read to her four times in a row.

In the last few months I have been on a course about observation as a learning tool (for me) and have started carrying a notebook around with me and jotting things down as I go along.

In terms of planning, well ... I don't write massive plans but I do think about what things to set up each day and do try and link this to what I have seen the children do and what I think they are interested in. For example, last week when I noticed Jojo's interest in building, I took both of the children I care for in the mornings for a walk to a local building site and Jojo was mesmerised, so the next day I took them into the garden and gave him some milk crates and he spent ages building things. It was wonderful for him but seemed to interest Hannah too.

I have just started a **Profile book** for each child and I put my notes in there plus my photos. I will give these to the parents when the children move on and they can take them to the nursery or school.

Roberto, teacher working at a children's centre

Roberto trained as a teacher and worked initially in a primary school and then in a nursery class before applying for a job in a children's centre. Here is what he said:

I work at a children's centre and when I started there they already had a very clear and open planning and recording system. I had worked in a nursery class before and very much enjoyed the more collaborative and collegiate approach in the children's centre. The head is trained in early years and keeps abreast of all developments and organises a very comprehensive programme of in-service training for us all. So we have been trained in how to observe children and record our thoughts; how to note significant leaps in learning; how to involve children commenting on their own development; how to involve parents in contributing to our records, and so on.

Each child has a folder and this is where we keep all the notes and records we keep on the child. Actually that is not quite true. We used to do that but these were getting so large that they were really not usable so each week we are asked to sift through and take out things that don't tell us anything new. We use sticky label Post-it notes and anyone who observed something just puts their notes or photos in the folder and in the weekly sift-through the key person reads through the loose Post-it notes and sticks in the ones that show something new. We have sections in the file for the learning areas and try and match the comments to these, although the match is not always accurate. That's because examples of learning often show just how holistic young children's learning is. The folders are stored in a low storage area so that children can reach them and put things in for themselves. One of the most positive things, for me, is to see a young child selecting a piece of work to go into the folder. These are always retained!

Sue, head of a children's centre

Sue trained as an early years teacher and then did a postgraduate degree where her area of special interest was in early years planning. As head of a children's centre she has organised programmes of in-service training for her staff, put in place an observation and planning system and involved parents in the life of the centre, and has been guest lecturer at many courses and conferences. This is what she said.

> I have introduced a system of keeping observation notes where, rather than using bits of paper and Post-it notes, each key person keeps an **observation diary** for each child in his or her group. These notes are often the ongoing, on-the-hoof and brief comments jotted down during the day but there are also more detailed observation notes, as when someone focuses on a particular child for a long period of time. Here is one such **detailed observation**:

>> Ade and Jemima both at the painting easels. Ade picks up thick brush and feels the bristles with his fingers and then runs the brush gently across his face. Then he rubs the brush on the paper and seems to listen to the sound it makes. The brush is dry. He feels it again and this time strokes his bare arm with it. Then he walks over to Jemima who is painting – dipping the brush in the paint and that on the paper. He very tentatively puts the brush in the tray of red paint and feels the wet paint-brush. Seems surprised that his fingers become red. Wipes them on his apron and then jabs the brush on the paper. A look of amazement on his face as red blobs appear on the paper. Dips the brush with the red paint still on it into the yellow paint tray and dabs it on the paper. Look of utter astonishment when orange blobs appear. Repeats the dipping and dabbing in two colours until the paper is completely covered and heavy with paint.

I noted that Ade is newly arrived in the country and new to the setting. He had clearly never painted on paper before or perhaps seen a paintbrush. He explored the brush with his fingers and his face and arm. He used Jemima as a model and copied what she did. He seemed to find the whole process of putting colour on paper fascinating and clearly noticed how the colour changed. He spent a very long time doing this.

We have learned from the system in place at Fortune Park Children's Centre, which we visited before we introduced our new system and where they use individual Profile books which start on the day of the initial visit to the child's home, before the child starts at the centre. We do that too, and keep these where the children can access them and try and record all aspects of learning in these. Parents are encouraged to contribute to them, as are children, and they are all different and very individual. They make for fascinating reading and offer a real window into the processes the child is going through from day to day and year to year.

Angelina, Foundation Stage Co-ordinator in a primary school Foundation Stage Unit

We became a Foundation Stage Unit about a year ago and are enjoying working as a fairly large team. Out intake is very mixed. We are a large inner-city school in Leeds and many of the children in the unit are plur-ilingual. We are committed to offering all the children a rich learning environment which recognises and respects the languages and cultures of all the children – and staff. The staff team is very mixed, and that is a real bonus because we have practitioners who can speak some of the languages of our children. I think we are starting to work really well as a team. All of us observe the children and use sticky-back paper for doing our quick observation notes. We use cameras, of course, and video sometimes, parti-cularly when we want to explain or share with parents. We have now star-ted collecting examples of children's work – their mark-making or drawing or painting or the models they make. We are taking care to annotate these to show why they have been chosen. Incidentally, either staff or children can choose things to go in. The images of children's learning which follow are some examples to entertain you.

We do involve the children and their parents in the assessment process. And we have put in place a system for checking and **reviewing the Profiles** or records we keep. We try and do this once a term, and what happens is

Example of children's learning: Bilal chose this to go into his folder.
He said, 'I drew bricks! And you can see my bed inside.'

Examples of children's learning: a two-year-old who was really interested in this handle
in a museum and seemed to be asking, 'What does it do? What can I do with it?'

Examples of children's learning: One child is modelling what an 'expert' painter does while the other watches. Learning through interaction!

Examples of children's learning: Zac and Jake made this tower at home and Jake fetched a ladder so that he could make it as tall as he wanted to.

that the key person and the child concerned review the child's record together, talking about things and about what they show. We believe this is important in getting the children to **reflect on their own learning** and development. Here is a transcript of what was said during one such 'conference'. The child concerned was three years old. We will call the practitioner Marcia and the child Precious.

Marcia: Did you like looking through your record?

Precious: It was good.

Marcia: What was the best thing you did?

Precious: That painting – my mum and me in the park.

Marcia: That was lovely. I really liked the colours you used.

Precious: Yeh – lots of black and red and that bluey colour.

Marcia: What do you think you are really good at now? [She is looking at a photograph of Marcia on the climbing frame.]

Precious: I can't climb really high – but that's because I am still little. My sister climbs high.

Marcia: But look how high you are in this photo.

Precious: But I can jump high. Did you get a photo of me jumping?

Denise and her views on assessment and planning

Denise has come in to work as an advisory teacher in an inner London borough after having trained as a teacher in New Zealand and been head of a Sure Start unit in Norwich. Here is what she said about her views on assessment and planning.

> I was trained in New Zealand and you have probably heard about Margaret Carr. She was famous in New Zealand, mainly for her work around the **Te Whariki curriculum** and around her approach to assessment and planning. I heard her talk about what she called 'the four Ds of assessment' and these were **describing, discussing, documenting** and **deciding**. I drew up this chart which I use when I give talks on assessment to teachers, practitioners and headteachers or heads of centre. I like having a process which seems clear and not too cumbersome and I know that some practitioners find this helpful.

The four Ds of assessment

I always start my talks by saying how important it is to foster positive attitudes and habits in young children. When we focus on what they can do rather than on what they cannot yet do, we are likely to encourage a **positive disposition** to learning. In this way we are likely to treat them as competent learners and build an attitude to learning which will last them throughout many years of schooling and beyond. The approach Margaret Carr encouraged was through writing narrative accounts or **Learning Stories** about the children's progress and development. So practitioners can write little accounts of where the learning took place, with whom, how the children interacted, what strategies they used, how well they communicated, and so on. And we always start with the child.

Stella Louis, in her book for this series *Knowledge and Understanding of the World*, gives many examples of wonderful, revealing, moving and humorous learning stories. Here are some to show just what a powerful tool observation is. We start with Kai, aged 33 months at the time:

> The practitioner observed Kai in the morning looking at a spider's web in the garden, which had early morning dew on it. The practitioner gave Kai a magnifying glass to aid his exploration and interest. Kai appeared to be intrigued by the patterns made by the tiny drops of water on the web. At times, Kai looked quite confused. He asked the practitioner if it had been raining, and she answered 'no'. Kai examined the spider web through the magnifying glass. Being very careful not to touch it he described to the practitioner what he could see. He pointed out that all of the web was covered with rain but some parts of the web had very large beads of dew and other parts had tiny droplets and that he thought that the spider was going to get wet when he went home later. Later that afternoon, the practitioner encouraged Kai to look at the web again. By this time, the tiny drops of water had disappeared. Kai asked the practitioner 'Where has the rain gone?'
>
> (Louis 2009, p. 50)

And here is Rahim, aged seven months:

> Rahim, aged seven months, was observed sitting upright on his child-minder's lap, using both of his hands to put his foot into his mouth. He appeared to be intrigued and motivated as he persevered with this repeated movement over and over again.
>
> (Louis 2009, p. 64)

And finally we have 26-month-old Joshua:

> Joshua, aged twenty-six months, was observed looking at wedding photographs in which he was a pageboy at his auntie Jackie's wedding. He playfully told the practitioner that his aunt got married and his Daddy got drunk. Joshua became quite serious and had on a stern expression. He said that his mummy was cross.
>
> (Louis 2009, p. 148)

A case study

Andover Early Years Centre is an oasis of green and calm in the middle of one of Islington's more depressing estates. It looked particularly alluring on the dark, grey May day on which I visited it for the first time. I had come to see an old friend and colleague, Birgit Voss, in her role as head of centre. The first thing to catch my eye was the evidence of the valuing of the languages of the children. My first contact with Birgit nearly twenty years ago had shown me how her own experience of being bilingual had determined her concern to value the languages, cultures and experience of the children and their families, and evidence of this was prominent throughout the centre.

The purpose of my visit was to talk to Birgit about planning. I wanted to know the impact of the EYFS on planning and practice and I wanted to know whether planning for babies and toddlers was different and separate from planning for older children. The centre caters for 54 children with places for 12 babies (from birth to the age of two), 12 toddlers (two to three years of age) and 30 three- to five-year-olds. The centre is open from 7.45 a.m. to 5.30 p.m. for 49 weeks a year. It closes only for bank holidays and for two weeks in the summer and one week at the end of the year. So the centre offers extended day care plus a core morning and afternoon session. As a consequence, you will realise that the staff sometimes work shifts, often are on different pay and conditions, and have come from varied experiences in terms of life, work and training. The children, too, come from a wide range of experience and lifestyle.

The building itself is low and home-like and all the rooms radiate from a central hall – very like the *piazze* found in the Reggio Emilia nurseries. Around the whole building are gardens, leading off from each of the rooms and brilliant with colour, equipment, pathways and levels and secret places. My first thought was that I would be happy for my baby or toddler or nursery child to go there because of the immediate sense of it being a world created around the emotional, sensory, intellectual and physical needs of children.

The staff plan based on their observations of the children. All members of staff are involved in observing children and noting their observations on Post-it notes. Each team meets regularly to share their observations and they base their weekly plans on this. In addition to this all staff are involved in doing **focused observations** of three children over a week. These are the material for the children's Profile books, which track their development over their lives in the centre. Looking at one of these books is a deeply moving experience, showing how each individual moves ahead – sometimes dramatically and sometimes more slowly. Each book contains written accounts by staff, comments from parents, 'awards' for things like sharing or tidying up or doing something else to be applauded, photographs, pieces of work, all dated and presented over a six-week period. At the end of that period that child has the opportunity to present the Profile book to her parents and her peers. At the centre there were photographs of the children sitting and smiling proudly as an adult showed the book to the children and talked about the child's achievements. The Profile books for the babies each start with photographs taken on the visit to the child at home prior to entry, and then there are photographs charting things that illustrate the unique child, the child in positive relationships, the child using things and people to make sense of the world and the child learning from all her experiences.

The centre works around very broad themes – like music or art – and Birgit explains that this is really a hook on which adults can plan particular things to interest and excite children. Planning is done on a weekly basis, and displayed in each of the rooms and in the babies' room there is a repeated phrase which delighted me, which read something like 'Follow the child.'

Birgit talked about routines and rituals in a way I had not heard before, seeing routines per se as really important to young children in establishing a calm and soothing environment in which the expected happens. Certainly, on the day I visited I heard no child cry or shout, no adult raise his or her voice and no altercations of any sort. For Birgit, one of the most important routines is that of separation or handover – the moment of parting from the parent or carer. She makes a point of being there each and every day to meet and greet the child and parent at the start of the day and doing the same thing at the end of the day. Apart from this and from sleeping, eating and being changed, the routines include goodbye rituals (waving goodbye to the parent); hugs and physical comfort; snack times; a lot of singing involving the names of the children or numbers or greetings, sometimes in English and sometimes in one of the many languages of the families at the centre. The routines affect all the children, although they are different, of course, for the older children. And it was pleasing to hear that there are times when all the children can come together indoors or out.

Birgit has prepared an attractive booklet for parents and in it is a section called 'How Do I Know My Child is Progressing?' This tells parents that the environment is arranged so that children can be observed doing whatever they choose to do, and that this is how those involved with the children know what they can do and are interested in. It talks of the Profile book and invites parents to a 'Target Child' meeting at which a summary of the child's progress is given, together with ideas for what might happen next. At this meeting key workers offer to record what parents have to say about the child's interests and needs and to include that in their planning. In this way each child has a special week when there is a strong emphasis on supporting or extending her learning.

Note: Andover Early Years Centre was sadly closed in early 2009.

The voices of parents

Hughes (2009) provides a wonderful example of how parents can give us a real view into the learning that goes on at home or in the local neighbourhood.

PSRN

Let me introduce you to Holly, who is two years old. This is how her parents have described some of her interest in counting and the language of numbers.

We had two cups on the table, and Holly said she would like 'both of them'. I asked her how many cups there were, but she was rather flummoxed by this question. We were also flummoxed that she knew 'both' was for two objects but didn't seem interested in the fact there were actually two of them.

Holly refers to couples as 'you two', so Holly's father and I can be addressed as 'you two' as can both her grandparents. I think this is just a phrase to her as she couldn't explain that she's saying it because there are two people.

When I was peeling an orange recently, Holly asked me if I was 'turning the orange inside out'. When I had finished, she wanted to share out the segments, so I tried a small experiment of counting a few with her. Together we were able to count that there were five, although she couldn't give me the answer when I asked afterwards. Holly then ate one of the segments, and I asked her to count them again. With great enthusiasm, she counted to five again!

(Hughes 2009, pp. 16–17)

You may have your own views about whether or not the child should have been urged to count, when counting the objects was clearly not what she was interested in or paying attention to.

What have you learned?

This has been a chapter made up of stories about some practitioners and their views and experience of assessment and planning. In essence it has been a chapter reinforcing some of the things already discussed in this book. The intention has been to show the common threads running through aspects of planning and assessment in different settings and also to show the variations between them.

Glossary

deciding: The last of the 4Ds in Margaret Carr's approach to assessment and planning; this means planning.

describing: The first of the 4Ds in Margaret Carr's approach to assessment and planning; this means observation and recording.

detailed observation: This is the sort of observation carried out in order to pay close attention to an aspect of a child's learning and development that may be causing concern or be very interesting. It is a more in-depth look than everyday observations.

discussing: The second of Margaret Carr's 4Ds, this is when the observations made are discussed by those involved with the child or children.

documenting: The third of Margaret Carr's 4Ds, this is what we call recording or keeping a record.

focused observation: This is a more detailed and in-depth observation focused on one child and carried out in order to learn more about some specific aspect of that child's learning and development.

Foundation Stage Unit: This is where nursery and reception classes in a school operate as one unit, covering the Foundation Stage.

Learning Stories: The ways in which progress is charted in New Zealand early years' settings.

observation diary: A way of storing the observations made in a book.

Profile book: A way of storing observations made in a book for an individual child

positive dispositions: Dispositions are habits of mind and positive dispositions are those to be fostered and encouraged. A positive disposition to learning would be one where the child enjoys learning and wants to do more of it.

reflect on own learning: *An aim of all educators must be to get learners to be aware of what they already know and can already do.* Reflecting on their own learning is just this.

reviewing Profiles: It is incredibly easy to collect much too much information in the form of observation notes or samples of work. *Reviewing Profiles is an essential part of any manageable system.* It is where, on a regular basis, each Profile is reviewed and only meaningful material – i.e. material which shows significant moments or progress – is retained. It is good practice to involve the child in this.

Te Whariki curriculum: The early years curriculum in New Zealand which was built on community involvement.

7 The Early Years Foundation Stage Profile

In this chapter we turn our attention to examining how both the spontaneous on-the-hoof observations and the more detailed observations, plus any other evidence you gather on a regular basis, can be used to create the EYFS Profile. This is the first statutory assessment to be made of children and it takes place in the final school year of the foundation phase. This means that the EYFS Profile is the official **summative assessment** of the foundation stage. The ongoing assessment you have been doing is known as **formative assessment**.

Formative assessment

The regular and spontaneous kind of assessment we all do all the time when working with children is known as formative assessment. According to the Encarta dictionary, the word 'formative' means 'important and influential, particularly in the shaping or development of character'. We often hear people talking about the formative years being the early years, during which it is believed character and personality are formed. Formative assessment is so called because it is thought that it can be used to plan to help the child move ahead in her learning and development. Earlier in this book we have talked about setting up an assessment system and highlighted just how much of the assessment is done as part of the ordinary daily routines. You watch and you listen and you make notes. You do this in the classroom or the garden or the playground or at dinnertime or during walks or outings or group activities. You are taking note of what you see and hear, and what makes you take note is that something seems different or important or interesting or revealing. Here is an example to illustrate this. It comes from Reggio Emilia:

> A child brought in a bus ticket after the long summer break and said that she had been to visit her grandmother and had seen 'lots of arms and legs'.

This little comment did not arise out of the blue. The system in the nursery concerned was to try and bridge the long summer gap when the children don't come to the nursery by giving each child a box and inviting them to put anything into the box which would remind them of what they did in the holiday when they return to the nursery. On the first day back the child cited in the example, when asked what the bus ticket reminded her of, gave the comment about arms and legs. The practitioner involved was bemused about the comment and decided to try and find out more in order to understand what it was that the child had been interested in. All those involved in the education of young children are called by the Italian word for teacher or educator – namely **pedagogista** – and share an absolute belief in children's abilities to use everything at their disposal to make sense of their world. In other words, they take for granted that young children are rich and powerful thinkers. The adults listen to the children and watch them, and then document all their individual or joint enterprises. By recording what is seen and heard and assessing this, they open up the possibilities for genuinely responsive ways of teaching. This means that instead of starting with some objective or outcome, educators start with what they have seen the children do and say and use this as the basis for planning what is to come. They respond to the lead given by the child.

The *pedagogista* involved went on to say that she had found out that the grandmother lived in a steep hillside town where the route to the beach involved walking down very narrow streets lined with tall houses. Knowing that helped her and will help you understand that the view for the small child was that of arms and legs. So the practitioner, through her own research about the child's holiday, gathered the evidence to understand a comment which had intrigued and baffled her. But that was not the end of the story. The practitioner talked to her colleagues and to the children and between them they decided that many of the children, when talking about a large group of people or a crowd, did not really understand what made a group of people a crowd. This was evident when children said things like 'she must have been in a crowd' or 'a crowd is lots of people all going in the same way' or 'a crowd is people who all look the same'.

Based on this the *pedagogista* decided to use the interest and experience of this one child as the starting point for a whole project where children explored the concept of 'a crowd'. She planned a number of experiences and activities to allow the children to experience crowds, represent crowds and explore the concept of 'crowd'. This is how the project developed:

The first thing they did was to visit the town square or *piazza* to look at a crowd and become part of a crowd. The adults who accompanied the children talked to them about how some people were going one way and others another; how some were old people and some children or babies; about how some people might be walking fast or sitting down and drinking coffee, or running around and playing. So the first step was the physical exploration of being in a crowd.

Back at the nursery the children were invited to draw one another sometimes from the front, sometimes from the back and sometimes in profile. The drawings were coloured in and photo-copied and then, after a discussion about the different heights of people, the children had the choice of using the photocopier to either shrink or enlarge their images. The cut-out images were stuck on card and placed on cardboard stands to allow them to 'stand' upright. The children then arranged the figures on a large base, representing a square.

There were other aspects of this project including children playing at being in a crowd or being left out of a crowd. The focus of the educators was to encourage children to express their ideas and their feelings in as many different ways as possible. They believed that learning is consolidated where children have opportunities to represent and re-represent (or represent again) their thoughts and feelings. So children can draw or model or act or sing or dance or construct something in order to explore ideas. They can use some of their 'hundred languages'.

You should be able to see the planning and the learning in this example. The alert adult responded to something said by a child and used that as the basis for planning a project to help that one child (and, by implication, many others) understand an abstract concept. The planning took account of the ages of the children and started with the physical and first-hand exploration of a crowd and then allowed the children to explore many things, including feelings (being in a crowd, being out of a crowd) and mathematical concepts (space, size, direction).

> In another of the nurseries one of the children said that the birds in the playground looked 'bored'. This developed into the children discussing what they thought would entertain the birds and they decided that the birds needed play equipment. They went on to talk about how they could make play equipment for the birds and how they would assess how successful their attempts had been. The children talked and made plans and designs on paper. They then constructed their designs using found materials and wood and decided to paint them in bright colours to make them more attractive to the birds. After a discussion with a practitioner they said they wanted to know how successful the project had been (in terms of whether the birds chose to use one or other of the pieces of equipment). To do this they decided to set up a rota of birdwatchers to count how many birds used the little swing, how many the roundabout, and so on.
>
> (Smidt, personal observation)

Throughout both of these projects the practitioners continued to listen and watch and to take notes about what they saw and heard. They were using their everyday practice to formatively assess the learning taking place and made changes in their plans regularly in response to this. They did, of course, know each child very well, having listened to and watched them over time, spoken to their parents and carers and kept track of what they had been doing over their history in the setting. In order to assess the progress of each child involved they had to ask, 'Has this child moved on? Do I have evidence that this child has learned something new? Perfected something? Come up with a theory? Represented and re-represented her ideas and thoughts and feelings?' The practitioners make judgements about individual children's learning and development through their knowledge about the child and about theories of child development. This kind of judgement is formative in the sense that it helps us plan what to do next.

Summative assessment

Summative assessment is assessment that happens after the learning has taken place and it is done at the end of something. It could be the end-of-year or end-of-term examinations or SATS, or a test following the children having been told to learn how to spell a list of words or to write a report on a project carried out during the term. You will all be familiar with summative assessments from your own schooling and will know that this kind of assessment – usually known as testing – can be frightening for some children. It is clear that often it gives just a picture of what a child can do on one day in one area of learning. The EYFS Profile is interesting in that it is summative assessment but made up out of formative assessments. All those involved with the care and education of our youngest children are asked to assess children regularly and keep notes on what they see and hear. These observation notes build into the Profile, which is the summing up of the learning that has taken place between birth (or the age at which a child joined a setting) and the end of the Foundation Stage, when the child moves on to Year 1 in a primary school.

The judgements made here may be normative, formative or outcomes-based. **Normative** judgements are those based on our knowledge of other children of the same age, at the same stage, doing the same task, for example. We often hear people using judgements like these when they say things like, 'Well, he is behind the others in his age group,' or 'She is reading like a seven-year-old.' There is an assumption here of what is normal. Some theorists, like Piaget, talk of ages and stages, assuming that learning and development are linear and straightforward. In fact, many people disagree with this view. You all know that all children are different and develop at different rates. A child's interests or home circumstances or health, for example, will certainly impact on how well he or she 'does' relative to other children. Normative judgements are informed by what it is thought other learners of the same age know or can do.

In our educational system we are increasingly asked to make judgements about a child in relation to some predetermined learning outcome or goal. So we might plan an activity for the children to do and have a set of learning outcomes in mind. These could include things like 'use a pair of scissors effectively' or 'demonstrate ability to accurately add two numbers together'. We would watch what the child does or what the child produces and then tick a box. Although this is a still-growing trend in early years education in this country, it is important to remember that in any situation the outcomes you have in your mind for what you want the children to learn may not match what the children want to learn. So this type of **outcomes-based assessment** gives an imperfect picture.

The National Assessment Agency has produced and published a series of short videos which illustrate the EYFS assessment scales and scale points. These are excellent and certainly worth watching. You can download them either without voice over or with voice over. Details of how to do this can be found in the Website section of the Bibliography. I do recommend that you take the time and trouble to do this. You will find it both entertaining and helpful.

How the EYFS Profile works

To help you understand how the EYFS Profile works, do read this transcript of part of a meeting held at a local professional development centre (PDC) to which those involved in or concerned about the EYFS Profile were invited. Present were parents, school governors, teachers and practitioners, an early years inspector and advisory staff from the PDC. The meeting was chaired by the head of a primary school.

Q: I am a parent and I want to know what this Profile is.

A: It is the way of summing up the progress of your child and all the other children at the end of the Foundation Stage and across all the learning areas. It is made up of 13 assessment scales and these are based on the early learning goals and the stepping stones. I am sure you have come across these.

Q: I am also a parent and I want to know what the purpose of this Profile is.

A: Well, a good question and one I am happy to answer. The Profile is the tool we propose to summarise what children have achieved during the years before entering Year 1 and to help the Year 1 teachers plan properly for the children they will be receiving. Also to give you, as a parent, details of your child's achievements.

Q: I am a childminder and I don't know what my responsibility is in terms of this.

A: As a childminder you are asked to observe the children in your care and build on what you already do. I am sure you already comment on what you learn about the children as you watch them and listen to them. What the EYFS asks you to do is to keep a record of your thoughts. You can do this through writing short notes or taking photographs to help you remember what you have seen and heard. You can also share these with parents. What you are doing is collecting evidence of children's progress to help the reception class teacher when he or she completes the Profile. It is completed in the child's last term of the Foundation Stage – so it will be the responsibility of those in the reception class to do this. But your notes will provide them with some of the evidence they need to do this well.

Q: I am a newly qualified teacher in the reception class and the thought terrifies me. What do I have to do?

A: You will have made observations of children's learning and built up individual learning books or Profiles and these give you the evidence you need. Now you use your own reporting systems in your school or the Foundation Stage Profile booklet or the eFile. Here you will find the 13 scales, each of which is divided into bands. You will find all the details you need in a document called *Continuing the Learning Journey* which is available from the National Assessment Agency. This is full of useful support and guidance – I should say especially useful to teachers wanting to know how to use the Profile to help them plan their Year 1 programmes.

Q: I am a practitioner in a children's centre and want to know on what basis judgements are made about the children.

A: Judgements are made based on ongoing observations and assessment of each child in all six learning areas. Each child's level of development must be recorded against the 13 assessment scales derived from the early learning goals. Judgements should be made from assessing children's behaviour and responses mainly through self-initiated activities – i.e. through play. The National Assessment Agency (NAA) recommends that at least 80 per cent of the evidence should come from what you observe the children doing through self-chosen activity, and the remaining 20 per cent from adult-directed or focused assessments. You should ensure that what you comment on is what you have seen the child do **consistently** and **independently**.

Q: Can you explain these assessment scales?

A: Yes – certainly. They are, as I said, derived from the early learning scales and within each scale there are three **progressive** bands. The first band is made up of Statements 1 to 3 and these relate to the stepping stones. The next band is made up of Statements 4 to 8 and these come from the early learning goals. Then the last point describes a child who is beyond the level of the early learning goals. In order for a child to reach this point, Point 9, they must have achieved all the Points 1–8 in that scale.

Q: I am a headteacher. Are the points **hierarchical**?

A: No. They focus on different aspects of development.

Q: I am a parent of a child with special educational needs. How will he be assessed?

A: Children who have special educational needs may require an alternative approach to assessment. I suggest you should seek the advice of whoever is responsible in your local authority.

Q: Can you tell me if I have any rights, as a parent, to contribute to the development of the Profile. I feel that I should, since she is my child.

A: A written summary which reports your child's progress against the early learning goals and the assessment scales must be sent to parents in the child's last term of the Foundation Stage. So the answer is yes, in the sense that you have the right to know what is being said about your child. In addition, parents do have the right to a copy of the actual Profile so you must be given a copy if you request one.

Q: I actually want to know if my views on how well my child is doing go into the Profile.

A: The guidance encourages practitioners to invite parents and children themselves to contribute, so I suggest you talk to the setting about this. We know that the views of both parents and children are really important.

Q: I am a reception class teacher and want to know exactly what I must do.

A: You have to complete the Profile by the end of the reception year, and to do this you need to record each item that the child has achieved in each scale. Make sure you consider each point separately. For each scale point, the judgement you make should represent your assessment of the child's typical attainment. This means that you will recognise that the child's performance may vary from day to day and from context to context. What you seek to do is to select what best describes the child's achievement.

Just a taste of what some of the levels look like

Thinking about what nine different levels might look like is an incredibly abstract task so here, just as a taster, we offer you some ideas of what different points on the eight-point scale look like in reality. We will examine some of the learning areas and in doing this we draw on materials prepared by the NAA.

You can see progression from Level 7 to Level 8 of PSED SD and also the links between social and emotional development and knowledge and understanding of the world in the particular examples in the following table.

Learning area	Scale	Point	FSP statement	To think about	What do the children need to demonstrate in order to attain this?	Cross-reference scale point evidence
PSED	SD	8	Understands that she can expect others to treat her or her needs, views, culture and beliefs with respect	Can you see that this is a move on from the one below – Point 7? The implication is that the child should not accept that she is wrong or inferior because she is different. She should be secure with their own experience and culture.	• Share their experiences and beliefs because they expect to get a positive reaction from adults and other children. • Identify themselves with specific resources, materials and displays in a positive way.	PSED SD7 PSED ED 6 KUW 6
PSED	SD	7	Understands that people have different views, cultures and beliefs that need to be treated with respect	This scale point is considering that others have different experiences and beliefs and that this is not a matter of conflict. There is no right or wrong.	• Be aware or differences, for example different kinds of music or food or art, etc. • Be able to express likes and dislikes and preferences in a way that is respectful of difference.	PSED 8 PSED 6 KUW 6

(Table continued on next page)

Learning area	Scale	Point	FSP statement	To think about	What do the children need to demonstrate in order to attain this?	Cross-reference scale point evidence
KUW		6	Finds out about past and present in own life and those of family members and other known people. Begins to know about own culture and beliefs and those of others.	This scale point is in two parts: ● The understanding of time and how things and people change over time. ● Understanding that different people have different experiences and beliefs.	● Be able to talk about and express examples of own cultural experience and able to share with others. ● Recognise other children's different experiences and show interest in this.	PSED SD 7 PSED SD 8 PSED 6 KUW 5
PSED	ED	6	Has a developing respect for own culture and beliefs and those of others.	This makes a judgement of the child's confidence with her own experience and an understanding that this may be particular to her. Also focuses on the understanding that the experiences of others may be very different. Respect is critical.	● Be able to talk about and express examples of her own cultural experiences and a willingness to share with others. ● Recognise other children's different experiences and show interest in this.	PSED SD 7 PSED SD 8 KUW 6

Notes: The key to understanding this: PSED means Personal Social and Emotional Development; SD means Social Development; ED means Emotional Development; KUW means Knowledge and Understanding of the World.

What you have learned

In this chapter we have looked at what happens at the end of this, the initial stage of learning, and at how teachers working in reception classes have the responsibility to complete the EYFS Profile. This is the first form of summative assessment for these very young children and follows the child into the first year of Key Stage 1. Your role is to continue to observe children, record your ideas and findings and keep records, based not on external outcomes but on what you have seen and heard the children say and do. You may, of course, have carried out more in-depth observations where you are looking at or for something specific. Your role as educated observer – 'educated' in the sense that you have some understanding of what is currently thought about how young children learn and develop best – is crucial. You are the most importer collector of evidence.

Glossary

consistently: This means regularly and more than once.

formative assessment: The type of assessment you do all the time.

hierarchical: Organised according to importance or significance.

independently: This means alone and without help. It is what the child can do alone.

normative assessment: The type of assessment which considers what is 'normal' for a cohort of children. So you might read of what is 'expected' of all five-year-olds. We know that all children learn at different rates so this is not a reliable type of assessment.

outcomes-based assessment: The type of assessment which measures a child's performance against a predetermined goal.

pedagogista: The Italian word for teachers or educators (practitioners, in our world).

progressively: One following the other, from simple to complex.

summative assessment: The type of assessment that comes at the end of a term or a topic or a stage or a phase and sums up the child's achievements to date.

A final word

This series of books has been written in advance of the start of the EYFS and it will be interesting to see how adequately the books address the many issues currently being faced by all those involved. I do hope that this small book on planning will be of help to those of you new to doing this and that it will help you keep in mind the importance of your own experience and views. Do not disregard these or be persuaded that they are not vital. They are. You have been working with children perhaps for many years and many of the things you are being asked to do formally are things you may have done instinctively just because you are interested in and care about the children. Try and find ways of minimising the amount of time (and paper and trees!) involved in all the new regulations and continue to hold tight to a belief in starting from the child. Good luck!

Bibliography

Note: The asterisk (*) indicates work by the key influences cited on page 17.

*Athey, C. (1990) *Extending Thought in Young Children*. London: PCP.

Bradford, H. (2009) *Communication, Language and Literacy in the Early Years Foundation Stage*. London and New York: Routledge.

Bromley, H. (2006) *Making My Own Mark – Play and Writing*. London: Early Education.

Brown, B. (2001) *Combating Discrimination: Persona Dolls in Action*. Stoke-on-Trent: Trentham Books (www.persona-doll-training.org).

—— (2008) *Equality in Action: A Way Forward with Persona Dolls*. Stoke-on-Trent: Trentham Books.

*Bruce, T. (1991) *Time to Play in Early Childhood Education*. Sevenoaks: Hodder and Stoughton.

*Bruner, J.S. (1966) *Towards a Theory of Instruction*. London: Harvard University Press.

—— (1980) *Under Five in Britain*. London: Grant McIntyre.

—— (1997) 'Celebrating Divergence: Piaget and Vygotsky', *Human Development* 40: 63–73.

Conteh, J., Martin, P. and Robertson, L.H. (eds) (2007) *Multilingual Learning: Stories from Schools and Communities in Britain*. Stoke-on-Trent, UK, and Sterling, USA: Trentham Books.

DfES (2003) *Foundation Stage Profile: Handbook*. London: DfES.

—— (2007a) *Statutory Framework for the Early Years Foundation Stage: Setting the Standards for Learning, Development and Care for Children from Birth to Five*. Nottingham: DfES.

—— (2007b) *Practice Guidance for the Early Years Foundation Stage. Every Child Matters: Change for Children*. Nottingham: DfES.

—— (2008) *Practice Guidance for the Early Years Foundation Stage*. London: DfES.

*Donaldson, M. (1978) *Children's Minds*. London: Fontana.

*Dunn, J. (1988) *The Beginnings of Social Understanding*. Oxford: Blackwell.

*Goldschmied, E. and Jackson, S. (1994) *People Under Three: Young Children in Day Care*. London and New York: Routledge.

Gooch, D.T., Powell, K. and Abbott, L. (2003) *Birth to Three Matters: A Review of the Literature*. London: DfES.

Goodman, Y. (1986) 'Children Coming to Know Literacy', in W. Teale and E. Sulzby (eds) *Emergent Literacy: Writing and Reading*. Norwood, NJ: Ablex.

Goleman, D. (2004) *Goleman Omnibus. Emotional Intelligence and Working With Eq*. London: Bloomsbury Publishing PLC.

*Gregory, E., Long, S. and Volk, D. (eds) (2004) *Many Pathways to Literacy: Young Children Learning with Siblings, Grandparents, Peers and Communities*. London: RoutledgeFalmer.

Gretz, S. (1981) *Teddy Bears' Moving Day*. London: Ernest Benn.

*Gura, P. (1992) *Exploring Learning: Young Children and Block Play*. London: PCP.

Harste, J.C., Woodward, V.A. and Burke, C.L. (1984) *Language Stories and Literacy Lessons*. Portsmouth, NH: Heinemann Educational Books.

Hughes, A.M. (2009) *Problem Solving, Reasoning and Numeracy in the Early Years Foundation Stage*. London and New York: Routledge.

Hutchin, V. (2007) *Supporting Every Child's Learning Across the Early Years Foundation Stage*. London: Hodder Education.

*Katz, L. (1988) 'What Should Young Children Be Doing?' *American Educator*, Summer: 28–45.

*Kenner, C. (2004) *Becoming Biliterate: Young Children Learning Different Writing Systems*. Stoke-on-Trent: Trentham Books.

Kress, G. (1997) *Before Writing: Rethinking the Paths to Literacy*, London: Routledge.

Laevers, F. (1994) (ed.) *Defining and Assessing Quality in Early Childhood Education*. Belgium: Leuven University Press.

Lancaster, L. (2003) 'Moving into Literacy: How It All Begins' in N. Hall, J. Larson and J. Marsh (eds) *Handbook of Early Childhood Literacy*. London: Sage.

Long, R. (2005) *Children's Thoughts and Feelings*. London: David Fulton Publishers.

Louis, S. (2009) *Knowledge and Understanding of the World in the Early Years Foundation Stage*. London and New York: Routledge.

McKee, D. (1996) *Not Now, Bernard*. London: Red Fox Books.

*Malaguzzi, L. (1984) 'L'Occhio Se Salta Il Muro'. Report on education in the *scuole comunali dell'infanzia* in Reggio Emilia.

May, P. (2009) *Creative Development in the Early Years Foundation Stage*. London and New York: Routledge.

*Moyles, J. (ed.) (2007) *Early Years Foundations: Meeting the Challenge*. Maidenhead: Open University Press.

Nurse, A.D. (2009) *Physical Development in the Early Years Foundation Stage*. London and New York: Routledge.

*Nutbrown, C. (1994) *Threads of Thinking: Young Children Learning and the Role of Early Education*. London: PCP.

Parker-Rees, R. (2007) 'Liking to be Liked: Imitation, Familiarity and Pedagogy in the First Years of Life', *Early Years* 27: 3–17.

Piaget, J. (1952) *The Child's Conception of Number*. New York: The Humanities Press.

Piaget, J. and Inhelder, B. (1969). *The Psychology of the Child*. New York: Basic Books.

Rinaldi, C. (2006) *In Dialogue with Reggio Emilia: Listening, Researching and Learning*. London and New York: Routledge.

*Rogoff, B. (1990) *Apprenticeship in Thinking: Cognitive Development in Social Contexts*. Oxford: Oxford University Press.

Sheppy, S. (2009) *Personal, Social and Emotional Development in the Early Years Foundation Stage*. London and New York: Routledge.

Siegler, R.S. and Alibali, M.W. (2005) *Children's Thinking* (3rd edition). New Jersey: Pearson Prentice Hall.

*Siraj-Blatchford, I., Sylva, K., Muttock, S., Gilden, R. and Bell, D. (2002) *Researching Effective Pedagogy in the Early Years*, DfES Research Brief 356. London: DfES.

Smidt, S. (1998) *The Early Years: A Reader*. London and New York: Routledge.

—— (2005) *Observing, Assessing and Planning for Children in the Early Years*. London and New York: Routledge.

—— (2006) *The Developing Child in the 21st Century: A Global Perspective on Child Development*. London and New York: Routledge.

—— (2007) *A Guide to Early Years Practice* (3rd edition). London and New York: Routledge.

Sroufe, L.A. and Wunsch, J.P. (1972) 'The Development of Laughter in the First Year of Life', *Child Development* 43: 1326–44.

*Tizard, B. and Hughes, M. (1984) *Young Children Learning*. London: Fontana.

Trevarthen C. (2001) 'Intrinsic Motives for Companionship in Understanding: their origin, development and significance for infant mental health'. *International Journal of Infant Mental Health*, 22(1–2): 95–131.

Underdown, A. (2006) *Young Children's Health and Well-being*. Maidenhead. Open University.

*Vygotsky, L. (1967) 'Play and its Role in the Mental Development of the Child', *Soviet Psychology* 5: 6–18.

—— (1978) *Mind in Society: The Development of Higher Psychological Processes*. Cambridge MA: MIT Press.

*Wells, G. (1986) *The Meaning Makers: Children Learning Language and Using Language to Learn*. Portsmouth: Heinemann.

White, J. (2002) *The Child's Mind*. London: RoutledgeFalmer.

Wilcock, L. (2000) *The Early Years Foundation Stage in Practice*. London: Step Forward Publishing.

Websites

Birth to Three Matters: www.surestart.gov.uk/resources/childcareworkers/birthtothreematters

Continuing the Learning Journey: www.standards.dcsf.gov.uk/eyfs/resources/ downloads/qca-05-1590_cont_lj.pdf

The Effective Provision of Pre-School Education (EPPE): www.kl.ioe.ac.uk/ schools/ecpe/eppe/

Every Child Matters: Change for Children: http://everychildmatters.gov.uk/

Foundation Stage: www.surestart.gov.uk

National Assessment Agency: www.naa.org.uk

The Standards Site: www.standards.dcsf.gov.uk

TeacherNet: www.teachernet.gov.uk

For additional documentation try emailing online.publications@comms.dcsf. gov.uk

Index

Chapter heading are in **bold**. Learning Areas are in *italic*.